27 VIEWS OF ASHEVILLE

RIVERSIDE CEMETERY

APPALACHIAN TRAIL

CHEROKEE

WOLFE HOUSE

BLACK MOUNTAIN

FRENCH BROAD RIVER

THE GROVE ARCADE

VANCE MONUMENT

CITY HALL

YMI CULTURAL CENTER

BILTMORE HOUSE

# 27 VIEWS OF ASHEVILLE

A Southern Mountain Town in Prose & Poetry

Introduction by Rob Neufeld

eno
publishers

*27 Views of Asheville: A Southern Mountain Town in Prose & Poetry*
Introduction by Rob Neufeld
© Eno Publishers, 2012

Eno Publishers
P.O. Box 158
Hillsborough, North Carolina 27278
www.enopublishers.org

ISBN-13: 978-0-9832475-1-7
ISBN-10: 0-983-2475-1-X
Library of Congress Control Number: 2011938339
Printed in the United States
10 9 8 7 6 5 4 3 2 1

Cover illustration by Daniel Wallace, Chapel Hill, North Carolina
Design and typesetting by Horse & Buggy Press, Durham, North Carolina

# Acknowledgments

Eno Publishers wishes to acknowledge the generous support of the North Carolina Arts Council's Arts and Audiences grant which helped fund the publishing of *27 Views of Asheville*.

The publisher also wishes to thank Gita Schonfeld, Katie Saintsing, Adrienne Fox, and Spencer Woodman for their careful editorial work on the views, and Daniel Wallace — writer, artist, friend — for his colorful rendering of Asheville.

A huge thank you to our twenty-seven writers and Rob Neufeld who have created a literary montage of Asheville, now and then.

# Permissions

Some of the works in this volume have appeared in whole or in part in other publications.

Robert Morgan's poem, "Milkshake," originally appeared in the publication *Fresh* (2010).

A version of Heather Newton's story, "House of Twigs," appeared in *Wellspring* and in *Irons in the Fire: Stories from the Flatiron Writers*.

Sharyn McCrumb's story, "Baghdad on the French Broad," is based on material from her novel, *Ghost Riders* (reprinted by John F. Blair, Publisher) copyright © 2012.

"Sabbath Day at McCormick Field," by Allan Wolf, originally appeared in the *Asheville Citizen-Times*.

"McCormick Field," by Michael McFee, appears in his book, *That Was Oasis* (Carnegie Mellon University Press), copyright © 2012.

"Chicken Hill," by Holly Iglesias, was originally published in *Angles of Approach* (White Pine Press), copyright © 2010.

Ron Rash's poem, "The Wolves in the Asheville Zoo," originally appeared in his book, *Among the Believers* (Iris Press), copyright © 2000.

George Ellison's essay, "Beautiful World, Farewell," is in part adapted from his newspaper columns and *High Vistas* (Vol. 1).

Glenis Redmond's poem, "Footnotes," originally appeared in *Appalachian Heritage* (Vol. 36, No. 3, Summer 2008).

Sarah Williams's story, "Vote," is excerpted from her novel, *Backside of the Country* (PublishAmerica), copyright © 2007.

Wayne Caldwell's story, "Rattlesnakes": copyright © 2011 Owlhead Inc.

Thomas Rain Crowe's "A Mountain Garden" is excerpted from *Zoro's Field* (University of Georgia Press), copyright © 2005.

# Table of Contents

## SENSING BOUNDARIES

## A PLACE CALLED HOME

## ⚜ VIEWS IN FICTION

## ⚜ THE HILLS BEYOND

# Preface

27 VIEWS OF ASHEVILLE is exactly that—twenty-seven perspectives of life in the much-storied Southern mountain city. The views span neighborhoods, decades and generations, and racial, religious, and cultural experiences, to create a sense of Asheville.

Some of the views celebrate Asheville; others expose its complicated past and complicated present. Some shine a lens on a community evolving; others on the price of that change; still others on the imperative of change. Some writers describe its urban landscape; others the hills beyond. And then there's Thomas Wolfe, whose genius informs many of the views herein.

*27 Views of Asheville* is not a guide in any traditional sense. It is more a literary montage: a composite made from a variety of genres—fiction, essays, poems—from a variety of writers. Our hope is that the book creates a sort of genius loci, giving readers insight into life in Asheville today and in the past, and into how twenty-seven of its inhabitants think about their home.

*Elizabeth Woodman*
Eno Publishers | Spring 2012

*Introduction*

## Alternate Histories

I REMEMBER, YEARS AGO, TELLING SOMEONE that I was writing a piece entitled "The Literature of Madison County," and they thought I was making a joke. Evidently, Madison's world-renowned ballad and story-telling traditions were not starred items in that person's library. Nor was there awareness of the renaissance out there.

That skeptic's view came from Asheville, looking out. It was not "a view of Asheville," yet it reflects the turbulence of creative movements, including country and urban influences, that mix in the city today. Traditions have overflowed divisions to foment—should we call it a "renaissance"? I think that's a useful description of what's going on here. A closer look reveals waves and currents.

The 1980s and 1990s growth in Asheville's literary prominence stemmed from the hills. Young people with writers' imaginations, inspired in some cases by Thomas Wolfe, matriculated from school systems that encouraged local voices. Parents sent their kids to colleges to study literature and write. Appalachian Studies programs emerged.

Fred Chappell grew up within the flood zone of Champion Paper and Fibre Company in Haywood County, went to Duke University, and studied under William Blackburn, who also taught William Styron and Reynolds Price. Later, as a teacher of writing at UNC–Greensboro, and today, as a full-time writer, he has served as a mentor to many up-and-coming writers.

In Chappell's fourth novel, *The Gaudy Place*, Arkie, a young teenage street hustler, ambles down Gimlet Street "past remnant goods stores, secondhand furniture stores, past dingy newsstands, upholstery shops, [and] sandwich factories" into "mule territory," where farmers sell produce off truck beds. Arkie wishes he got a cut of the protection money that Burn Ryan got from the farmers. He heads into the Lucky Star to con a dollar from a gullible "mule."

This is a sardonic, fictional view of 1950s Lexington Avenue in Asheville.

Clemmie, the hooker in the same book, uses her extra earnings to shop at Penney's, Woolworth's, Ivey's, and Belk's department stores, which once had formed the heart of downtown Asheville, but are now all gone. She walks past the "miniscule triangular park filled with people waiting for buses." That's our Pritchard Park, no longer a bus stop. The city has moved that function off the main drag to Coxe Avenue.

Put the ghost town behind you. Chappell did when *The Gaudy Place* met a chilly reception. He went on to write the landmark book of poetry, *Midquest* (1981); and, in the 1990s, his four Kirkman novels, which take place in mythologized Haywood County.

You can travel back further in Asheville history through the fiction of its great writers.

John Ehle places us in a version of 1910s Market Street in his novel, *Lion on the Hearth*; and continues through the Crash in *Last One Home*. Wilma Dykeman takes us to the farmers' and tobacco markets of the nineteenth century in *The Tall Woman*. Sharyn McCrumb hangs a shingle in Civil War Asheville in *Ghost Riders* and *The Ballad of Tom Dooley* (read her Zebulon Vance piece in this volume).

You can also travel out farther, geographically.

In 1995, poet Robert Morgan published the novel, *The Truest Pleasure*; and in 1999, *Gap Creek*, recreating the world that he had known as a boy growing up on a Henderson County farm. His father used to hang out by a fence rail and talk about Jefferson with neighbors.

Morgan, the son, established the country as the center of interest with his poems about farm work, descriptions of pioneer life, and stories of struggle and religion. Guy Moore, his writing teacher at N.C. State, had advised him, "Write about the place and people where you grew up."

Asheville was Oz, as Morgan's poem in this collection shows. Today, conservative critics dub Asheville a "cesspool of sin"; new urbanites call it one of the great places for creative people to live. For Morgan and fellow country authors, the city was a bazaar and a museum.

Not just a museum, as in the case of Ron Rash's poem, "The Wolves in the Asheville Zoo," but a manifestation of doom. And not just a bazaar, as in Charles Frazier's piece, "Random Asheville Memories circa Mid-Twentieth Century," but a strange new territory, as vivid as boys' adventures stories. Frazier creates an alternate view of *The Gaudy Place* and the Eisenhower-Kennedy years in Asheville. "It was all downtown then," he says with astonishment, looking back on the pre-mall and pre-Beaucatcher-Cut city.

Gail Godwin views Asheville in Wolfe's wake, a terrain she drank in; and describes the city today as a retro-version of its 1920s' self.

For example, contemporary Asheville, with its love of cosmopolitanism, reveres architect Douglas Ellington's Art Deco influence.

When the city built its new Public Works Building on South Charlotte Street in 1993, architect Carroll Hughes's SPACEPLAN emulated Ellington's 1927 Asheville City Hall. In addition to providing space for garages and trucks near its offices, the architect designed the Public Works Building to serve as a gateway to the city, with street-side walls that looked better than highway barriers. The colors and patterns were Ellingtonesque; and the firm kept costs down by using big blocks of cheaper material to get the effect. Nonetheless, local scoffers dubbed the project "Taj Mah-garage."

Like SPACEPLAN, cultural leaders evoke Asheville's Golden Age to enliven the current renaissance. Thomas Wolfe, F. Scott Fitzgerald, O. Henry, and Carl Sandburg get banner treatment.

Only one of those writers cared much about Asheville; and, of course, that one's caring was all-encompassing. The other three produced scant region-related writing.

In his high society days, F. Scott Fitzgerald stopped in Asheville. In *The Great Gatsby*, his narrator, Nick Carraway, sees Jordan Baker and figures out "why her face was familiar—its pleasing contemptuous expression had looked out at me from many rotogravure pictures of the sporting life at Asheville and Hot Springs and Palm Beach."

A generation earlier, O. Henry had entered the already-glittering mountain burg with Sara Coleman, his childhood sweetheart from Greensboro, and now his second wife. Sara took him to her father's place in the mountains, in part to help him heal from the stresses of a lionized career.

The couple honeymooned at the famous resort in Hot Springs (then called Warm Springs) in Madison County. "Are you bored?" Sara asked.

"These are the happiest days I've had in many years," O. Henry replied.

He rented an office in the National Bank Building, later called the Sondley Building, overlooking Patton Avenue, the city's main artery. When the bank building had been built in 1891, it had been the pride of commercial downtown. In 1895, its architect, A.L. Melton, was hired to build a competing building across Church Street. Called the Drhumor, after the ancestral town of its owner, William Johnston, it made the bank building look second-hand next to its proud turret and its frieze sculpted by Biltmore Estate's Fred Miles. The bearded face that Miles placed on the side that faced the bank building was that of C.T. Deake, the florist who liked to gaze at him from the street level of the bank.

In 1976, the Sondley Building was torn down for a parking lot. The Drhumor Building survives, with altered entrance and sans turret, but with frieze preserved.

In O. Henry's few months in his office, he witnessed out his window a clash of pedestrians, horse-drawn carriages, and automobiles; and, at night, throngs at the Asheville Opera House, illuminated by the electric street lights that had given Patton Avenue the nickname, "The Great

White Way." The city was, as railroad promoters had begun to say, the "Paris of the South."

Yet, for O. Henry, hounded by producers of his play in Manhattan, it was not the place to be. It wasn't just that the author of "The Four Million" — about New York City's inhabitants — could not take to his newly embraced forty thousand in the mountain city. O. Henry, damaged by alcohol, was at the end of his life.

In his Asheville office, Sara Porter recalled, her husband "hung out of the window most of the day watching the crowds with a far-away look in his eyes, trying in vain to recapture the spark that would give life to his plots."

His doctor, William Pinkney Herbert, visited him at his workplace, and, as he noted in a 1971 issue of *Our State* magazine, observed its spartan character: "One room, a table, a mirror, a chair, an electric light hanging from a cord, a wash basin with a cold water spigot, occasionally a bag of oranges, a dictionary, an almanac, a yellow pad, pencils, and a waste paper basket — often full."

In 1910, O. Henry traveled to New York for his play and soon after died of a diseased kidney. Sara would not allow his remains to be sent to Greensboro, but had him buried in Riverside Cemetery in Asheville.

Carl Sandburg moved from Illinois to Flat Rock, North Carolina, in 1945, when he was sixty-seven. He bought "Rock Hill," the former estate of Christopher Gustavus Memminger, secretary of the treasury for the Confederacy, and renamed it Connemara. Flat Rock was and is a remarkable survivor of pre–Civil War Henderson County; and, though many old mansions remain private, the annual house tour by Historic Flat Rock has much to show.

Sandburg moved in after the huge success of his six-volume biography of Abraham Lincoln. Like O. Henry, he lived during his fame.

While his wife, Paula Steichen Sandburg, managed her prize Chikaming goats, Carl tended to poems and songs, and wrote the novel, *Remembrance Rock*, based on his Galesburg, Illinois, boyhood home. When Sandburg died, in 1967, his ashes were transported back to Remembrance Rock.

Riverside Cemetery is Remembrance Rock for many Asheville spirits. It's curious how many times the place comes up in this volume—for instance, in George Ellison's piece about the early nineteenth-century botanist, John Lyon, who's buried there.

"Asheville became his home away from home," Ellison writes about Lyon, who had made seven trips to Western North Carolina to collect plants; he had sent England what had been considered "the greatest collection of American trees and shrubs ever brought."

It appears that when we reach down alongside the Ellington vein to find more evidence of essential Asheville, we find our hands in roots.

"Whatever else it may claim to be," Ellison concurs, "the city has always been defined by the ready access it provides to scenic views and a diverse flora unsurpassed in the temperate regions of the world."

Geography is one reason that nature and environmental writers flourish here. Many of them have formed a kind of collective, appearing together at programs and in publications along with native authors who mourn and warn against the destruction of traditional ways.

Wayne Caldwell connects concern about traditional ways with downtown preservation in his story, "Rattlesnakes," included in this book. The narrator, "Rass" Carter, a character from *Cataloochee*—Caldwell's novel about a mountain community evicted by the National Park Service—tells how he'd become an Asheville lawyer representing a group fighting a downtown mall project.

The story mirrors actual events. In 1981, Strouse Greenberg Company of Philadelphia made plans, with political help, to raze the brick buildings that compose the Lexington Avenue/Market Street/Broadway district. That's Ehle territory, the place where country farmers had once brought their carts; and, more recently, where merchants such as Caldwell, a furniture man as well as a literature scholar, had filled out the practical side of the Asheville dream.

When my wife and I came to Asheville in 1988 to start a family, I became tour guide for the Preservation Society of Asheville and Buncombe County, a group that had helped limit the demolition of Pack Square to the north side. On that site, Akzona built its I.M. Pei Architects headquarters, with basement parking lot and rooftop park; a street-level floor with no retail; and reflective glass shielding the interior from view.

Caldwell's group, Save Downtown Asheville, soon after the Akzona project, brought together preservationists and merchants to stop the spread of renewal from the high-rent core to its commercial corpus.

"Ottis Green," I liked to say in a Believe-It-or-Not moment when my tour reached Caldwell's district, "had a hardware store at 11 West Pack Square in the 1920s — and a branch just three blocks away at Lexington and Walnut! The first was for the hotel crowd; and the second for locals."

A border existed between country and city, even in the city; and the edge persists. You can hear the edge when Rass comments about the mall, "I hadn't smelled such rotten fish since our last urban renewal." And you can hear it in Daniel Pierce's piece, "Hallowed Ground," about the Asheville Motor Speedway.

Preservationists did not jump to the rescue of the noisy racetrack when its new owner sold it to RiverLink for the city to build what would become Carrier Park. Alliances shifted and the dividing line was drawn differently than with the Lexington Avenue district. Pierce vividly recreates the world of 1960s working-class Asheville; and condemns the renewers, whose vision, he points out, gratified the genteel and at times seemed disdainful.

*27 Views of Asheville* reveals the multiple identities of Asheville. Alternate histories co-exist.

There are country people who have made a home in the urban sprawl, such as Uncle Victor in Pamela Duncan's story, "Chance Two." Uncle Victor's got some wisdom and has a role to play. And there's Richard Chess's view in his essay, "A Circle with No End." Chess strives to bridge the gap between Asheville-of-the-giant-cross on the one hand, and the Jewish culture of Israel on the other. The poet, Amichai, plays a major part in Chess's high note.

23

There is also the African American view. In Asheville, it is distinct. Historians like to point out that, here, going way back, African Americans had not been field workers, but craftsmen, hotel employees, and household workers; then with Emancipation, merchants and professionals. When the federal government instituted urban renewal in the Fifties, Sixties, and Seventies, Asheville had been one of the cities most devastatingly hit by the destruction. One of its three largest African American communities, Burton Street in West Asheville, was half run over by the interstate. The other two, Southside and East End, vanished as if in a holocaust.

This is why I cringe when I hear boosters say, with some justification, "Asheville is remarkable in that it survives as it was in its golden age."

One's head goes dizzy thinking about the ways in which that statement is true and untrue. In 1937, the electric streetcar lines were pulled up for the urban renewal of that time: an economy built on buses. The Federal Post Office tumbled, yielding its site to Pritchard Park. A grand hotel on Pack Square came down for a bank parking garage. The 1950s-era stores fled; school buses took kids home, ending the use of city buses with stops downtown. Thomas Wolfe's birthplace (not his mother's boardinghouse) was turned to dust, along with most of his neighborhood, to make way for the interstate and civic development. O. Henry's block, dust. The stores that Thomas Wolfe's brother Grover visited on the north side of the square in "The Lost Boy"—dust. And East End, the lively, loving, church-going, large neighborhood that extended from today's YMI Building to Beaucatcher Mountain—it was there one day and, if you went away a little while, gone the next.

Who's doing the viewing when we consider views of Asheville?

Right now, with book in hand and city in sight or mind, it's you. And it's you at your present moment in time. I used to say, on my preservation society tours, that one could see history taking place—in many cases, visually—every day in the city. "How to Make a Tourist Attraction out of a Mixed Bag" might have been my slogan.

But what if your aim is to foster something deeper than the celebration of symbols of diversity? What if you want to do what Rick Chess advises in his essay; that is, focus on the man with the produce baskets rather than on the monument behind him?

Thomas Wolfe is raising his hand. As Dale Neal makes clear in his essay, "Altamont Always," a re-reading of Wolfe (particularly the 2000 release of his original manuscript, *O Lost*) reveals the core principles of a view-making, or literary, process.

Wolfe reached long into family pasts; heightened realism for satirical effect; and spoke for the outsider. He wrote memorable descriptions, experimented and pushed boundaries, and identified Asheville as a place, as Neal testifies, "where terrible angels walk among us."

A full view of Asheville involves, finally, the recognition that writers are writing about it a lot, and are part of the evolution. There's a danger of Asheville becoming a reality show; but there are also good indications that the thrust is to bring people together for healthy understanding.

*Rob Neufeld*
Spring 2012

**ROB NEUFELD** is the longtime book reviewer and local history writer for the *Asheville Citizen-Times*; and the editor of the journals of Gail Godwin, published by Random House as *The Making of a Writer* (Vols. 1 and 2), and the forthcoming third volume that will be titled, *Working on the Ending*. He is also the author of many other works for various audiences; a program presenter; and the creator of the website, "The Read on WNC." He lives in Asheville with his wife and family.

# Looking Back ❧

# Thomas Wolfe's Asheville

GAIL GODWIN

WHY HAS THOMAS WOLFE'S ASHEVILLE been able to hold on for so long in the real place?

There's the terrain—a town ringed by mountain ranges. "The hills that shut in Altamont" were the incubus of Wolfe's "dark miracle of chance" (*Look Homeward, Angel*).

Wolfe wrote from his senses. He imposed his descriptions of Asheville— the streets, the trains, the speech—on what was already there. He saw it, heard it so truly and vividly that it seemed afterward to people who had not looked or listened as closely that he was simply saying what they had always felt.

"All through the ghostly stillness of the land, the train made on forever its tremendous noise, fused of a thousand sounds," George Webber muses in *You Can't Go Home Again*. "He remembered how these sounds, coming to him from the river's edge in the little town of his boyhood, had always evoked for him their tongueless prophecy of wild and secret joy, their glorious promises of new lands, morning, and a shining city."

Wolfe died young, just short of his thirty-eighth birthday. He was the age of the century and the year was 1938. His mother, relatives, teachers, and contemporaries had years and years more to live and keep his legacy going with their own stories.

My personal memories, for instance, include walking behind a man in a seersucker suit on Pack Square. My grandmother bends down and murmurs: "That's old _____. Tom Wolfe wrote about him in his book, and not too nicely."

During the war years, my mother was a reporter at the *Asheville Citizen*. She often went over with her notebook to Julia Wolfe's "Old Kentucky Home" whenever Tom's mother remembered something else important about her famous son.

My stepfather's father was in Tom's class at Claxton when they were boys. And the mother of the little girl I played with on Edwin Place worked as Wolfe's secretary in the summer of 1937, during his last visit to Asheville, when he rented a cabin out at Oteen. He was writing a long story about rich New Yorkers at a party just before the '29 crash. (This later became part of "The World that Jack Built" in *You Can't Go Home Again*.)

Much of the landscape of "Old Asheville," with its walkable Wolfe landmarks, was spared when the expressway was cut in the 1960s. Except for the razed neighborhood on the highway side of the Wolfe house and the construction of our new "skyscraper," a bank building on Pack Square, Wolfe's downtown stayed structurally the same.

During the Age of the Malls, which began with little Westgate in the early Sixties and spread outward in the other direction to the big malls in the Seventies and Eighties, downtown Asheville slumbered. Over the last twenty years, the city has revived into a retro-version of its old self. Some old things came into their own for the first time. The "Postal Accounts" building finally achieved its arcade glory denied it by the coming of WWII. Now, young, hip Ashevillians eat Cuban sandwiches on the street near the hotel that was once the home of Ivey's Department Store, the display windows of which were curtained on Sundays.

From the start, my relationship with Wolfe as a writer has had an added and complex dimension because we shared a hometown. I grew up on stories and legends about "Tom Wolfe," as most people in town called him: his voracious appetites for wine, women, food—and brawling; his gigantic stature, which had made it most comfortable for him to write standing up, using the top of his refrigerator as a desk; the voluminous output that flowed from his pen, gathered up by frantic secretaries to be typed up and packed into large crates.

When I was a child, Wolfe had only recently died of tubercular meningitis, which was diagnosed after an exhausting tour of the western United States. I had heard all the popular gossip about the local repercussions from his work long before I was old enough to read the novels (often morosely remarking to myself when I did read them, "He's used up so much of my material").

Shortly after *Look Homeward, Angel* was published, privately duplicated lists, identifying the characters in the novel (even very minor ones) with the real people on whom they were based, did a brisk business in Asheville. It was one of the things that led Wolfe to have George Webber lament, "You can't go home again." Implicit in his lament are the ways in which he *can* go home again. For, the artist and the poet in him would always be able to find home within the living word.

Asheville native **GAIL GODWIN** is the author of eighteen books, including the award-winning novels, *The Odd Woman, Violet Clay, A Southern Family, Evensong*, and, most recently, *Unfinished Desires*. She is recipient of a Guggenheim Fellowship and other grants and the Award in Literature from the American Academy and Institute of Arts and Letters. Three of her novels have been finalists for the National Book Award.

# Random Asheville Memories circa Mid-Twentieth Century

CHARLES FRAZIER

I WAS BORN IN BILTMORE VILLAGE, in the little hospital Douglas Ellington designed. But I grew up in Andrews, a small town surrounded by mountains two-and-a-half hours of winding mountain roads to the west. Because we had family near Asheville, we came east every couple of weeks. That was the late Fifties and early to mid-Sixties, the final years of Asheville before malls and sprawl and the 240 Bypass with its still-horrifying cut through Beaucatcher Mountain. From department stores to automobile dealerships, it was all still downtown then, and because the terrain discouraged a "Main Street" layout, Asheville's convoluted shape felt like a genuine small city rather than an overgrown town.

My cousins and I were fairly free-range children while my mother and her sisters were shopping, and I learned all the nooks and crannies of Asheville from our games of fox and hounds through the streets and stores. I liked the fox role and developed closely held secret routes reserved for times when the hounds drew near. Such as this one: Duck down Wall

Street and then up the steps to Battery Park; dash across the street into Penney's and up the escalator and immediately down the back stairs and outside again while the foxes searched through the store; then back to Wall Street and down to Pritchard Park via the stairway that I alone knew about. It never failed to shake them. After escaping a close call, the possibilities were endless. Patton, Coxe, Lexington, Broadway, Biltmore, Eagle. Of course you had to be careful not to run while inside the stores. Just walk fast and act like you're in Ivey's or John Carroll's or Winner's looking for your mother.

If my father was along, sometimes I'd go with him to the Man Store to watch him be fitted for a suit by a short, stocky tailor with a long tape measure draped around his neck and dangling to his knees. My father was a slim six foot four, so there was an innate Mutt & Jeff physical comedy at play. The tailor had probably known my father longer than I had and always called him Professor. Some time much later, while I was in college, I bought a suit there—or more likely, my father bought it for me—a pale summer item that the man with the tape called a Palm Beach suit. Which, in retrospect, makes me question my taste.

After I quit being a little kid and became a new-fledged teenager, I had shopping of my own to do. Asheville became my main source of culture, at least the kind of culture I found interesting: books, movies, music, bikes. I'd arrive on a Saturday morning in the back seat of my parents' car with a mental list and a few dollars saved from allowance and lawn mowing. I remember my best friend Mike's older brother, Larry, being a frequent source of suggestions. He was in high school and did lots of un-required reading and listened to folk music. I once spent a precious two dollar bill on a Kingston Trio record at his recommendation, and when Larry tossed off the comment that I should read *The Canterbury Tales*—I was maybe in the seventh grade—the title went to the top of my list. On my next trip to Asheville, I found a modern English version in the book department of Bon Marché, where I'd previously bought most of my Hardy Boys mysteries.

It was a little fat, square, green book. Daunting in many parts, but also occasionally interesting to discover how dirty and hilarious those olden people could be.

Bon Marché was only the beginning of my book circuit. I'd always go to Talman's on Wall Street and, at some point, to the Asheville Bookstore on Haywood Street. It was probably the first real bookstore I'd ever been in, and I still have a couple of slim books of poetry I bought there during high school: Sandburg and Eliot. I remember liking the somber tone of the place, the smell of new books, the strict logic of hardcovers upstairs and paperbacks down, the sibilant library hush of the salespeople and the customers. But I also liked the spinning wire racks of bright pulp paperbacks in busy drugstores and dime stores, and I especially liked the newsstand on College Street. It felt vast to me, and I was first drawn to its brilliant fanned array of comic books: *Batman* and *Superman,* of course, but also lesser lights like *The Flash* and *Green Lantern* and *Aquaman.* Later, after I'd given up comics, I went to the newsstand mainly for James Bond thrillers, and I remember getting in considerable trouble the week after I bought *On Her Majesty's Secret Service* because I couldn't prevent myself from reading it during eighth-grade English class.

It was about the same time, up at Pack Square at the Plaza Theatre, where I saw the first of the Bond movies, *Dr. No.* And also many others, before and after. Movies with special effects by Ray Harryhausen, fluffy comedies with Doris Day and Rock Hudson and Tony Randall, otherworldly Clint Eastwood spaghetti westerns, and most memorably, *Cool Hand Luke.* If I'd gone to a matinee, I'd walk out onto Pack Square blinking against the daylight as the known world reformed itself after two hours of full immersion in imagination.

At some point on a Saturday, I'd usually find myself at Merrill's Bike Shop on Commerce. It was dim and cavelike, with stone walls and tiny high windows, and it smelled of grease and rubber. Bikes — including stunningly expensive Paramounts — nearly filled the floor and dangled from the ceiling. I mostly went in for small parts and inner tube patch kits, but after the Austrian-made bike I had mowed lawns all summer long to buy was run over by an eighteen-wheeler—while I was on it—the shop managed to straighten the frame and build a new rear wheel to get me rolling again.

And of course there was always the crucial matter of lunch. When I was young, I held the opinion that a club sandwich was a sophisticated choice, so that's what I usually ordered at the counter in Woolworth's. If I went to the S&W, I tried to remind myself that French fries and mashed potatoes were not to be ordered together due to some arbitrary rule like not wearing white after Labor Day. In my teenager years, I preferred burgers at Cosmo's on Haywood, or chow mein at the Paradise on Broadway, where sometimes you'd catch a glimpse through the kitchen door of a slender old Chinese man with long wispy whiskers. The fact that my parents had gone to the Paradise on dates long before I existed made the place seem ancient and venerable, and the little jukebox stations in each booth contained song selections fading nearly back to the lost world of big bands and crooners.

I could go on and on. Such as the adventure of buying the first skateboard I'd ever seen in a store, though my pal Mike and I had already crafted homemade boards based on nothing but a picture in a magazine, *Life* probably. Or looking through the racks of singles in Woolworth's for the Zombies' "She's Not There," and that Beach Boys' "409" backed with "Surfin' Safari," two hits for the price of one. Also the Animals version of "House of the Rising Sun," though I had no idea then that it was a version and not an immediately overwhelming expression of contemporary genius. But the point is, for a kid from a small, isolated Southern Appalachian town in the mid-twentieth century, Asheville was a city of the American present moment, my point of access to all that immediate culture, the trash and the treasure. It was the place to find what's new.

Novelist **CHARLES FRAZIER** is the author of *Cold Mountain,* winner of the National Book Award. The novel was adapted into an Academy Award–winning film. Born in Asheville, Frazier is also the author of *Thirteen Moons* and, most recently, *Nightwoods.*

# Milkshake

ROBERT MORGAN

First time I heard of such a thing
I thought of milk stirred up to foam,
or beaten to a blue whipped cream.
And then at Asheville Dairy Bar
my first trip to that lofty city,
I watched the jerk with paper cap
dump things into a blender, churn,
then pour the contents in a cup
and bring to me. A straw, stabbed through
the frothy top, drew up a sip —
and never had I savored such
ambrosia, so cold it stung
my tastebuds and my tongue with grains
of ice and creamy essences,
and charged with flavor syrup on
the lips, the finest cold elixir
slurped in jubilation through
my teeth, across the mouth and down
the throat with plenty more to come,
unfreezing just enough to swill
like mother's milk of happiness,
and sap of future opulence,
all gold and frankincense and myrrh,
luxuriating mouth with thrill
of iced vanilla ichor, white
as julep of the angel host,
all mine for just two sweaty bits.

---

**ROBERT MORGAN** is the author of five novels, including *Gap Creek* and *Brave Enemies*, and numerous books of poetry and short stories. His nonfiction books include *Boone: a Biography* and, most recently, *Lions of the West: Heroes and Villains of the Westward Expansion.* He is the recipient of many awards, including the Academy Award in Literature from the American Academy of Arts and Letters. He is the Kappa Alpha Professor of English at Cornell University.

# Building Asheville

*The City's Arts & Crafts Heritage*

BRUCE E. JOHNSON

ASHEVILLE IS A CITY whose history can be read simply by walking its streets, strolling its neighborhoods, and exploring its architecture—from cabins to castles, bungalows to brick mansions, Arts & Crafts to Art Deco. Its architecture is as diverse, complex, and astonishing as most cities ten times its size. Amazingly, its buildings, downtown area, and neighborhoods did not truly begin to take shape until 1880, when, after several failed attempts to scale the surrounding mountains, the railroad finally arrived, opening the floodgates to a wave of outsiders who brought with them their ideas of how Asheville should be designed and developed.

Located in a lush valley formed by the merging Swannanoa and French Broad rivers, and surrounded by the Blue Ridge Mountains, Asheville first served as a crossroads and overnight stay for foot-weary settlers traveling west from Raleigh, south from Johnson City, and north from Greenville. Early attempts to scale the steep mountain slopes or blast tunnels through the granite fortress surrounding this mountaintop plateau were sabotaged by inexperience, political infighting, and blatant corruption. Eventually, however, the railroad was able to overcome the natural battlements guarding the peaceful valley, and Asheville began to blossom.

Word quickly spread of the natural beauty of this thirty-mile-wide valley and the medicinal remedies it offered: warm springs, clean air, cascading streams, and rocky waterfalls, friendly trails, mild winters, temperate summers, and lingering spring and fall seasons. Within three years of the arrival of the railroad, the mountain city's population doubled. Clapboard siding quickly replaced crude log cabins as the first of Asheville's renowned boardinghouses sprang up around Pack Square, where tourists began jostling their way past settlers, farmers, and drovers.

Among the newcomers was an aging Colonel Frank Coxe, bringing with him a legion of war stories that seemed to grow with each retelling. Standing an impressive six feet four inches tall and weighing more than two hundred and fifty pounds, Frank Coxe had grown up near Asheville, and as a young man had risen quickly through the ranks of the Confederate army to become a valued colonel.

When word reached him on the battlefield at Bull Run, however, that the United States government was about to confiscate his family's rich coalfields in Pennsylvania, Coxe hired a replacement to take his place in Kershaw's Brigade and headed north, traveling at night to avoid both Union and Confederate sentries, who were alert and anxious to shoot any deserters. Difficult not to notice, Coxe arrived in Pennsylvania where recruiters quickly attempted to draft him into the Union army. He warily invoked his legal right to again hire a replacement to fight in his place.

Before long, both the Union army and the Confederates suspected Coxe of being a spy, prompting him to flee to Europe until the Civil War ended. Upon his return in 1865, Coxe discovered that both of his hired replacements had been killed fighting on opposite sides in the same battle on the same day. Convinced they had shot each other, he reportedly boasted for years afterward that he was the only man in the Civil War who was killed twice in the same day, yet lived to talk about it.

Insensitivity aside, Colonel Coxe provided Asheville with its first major hostelry, the Battery Park Hotel. Built in 1886 on the highest downtown knoll, it was hailed as the finest hotel in all of North Carolina, featuring early Edison lighting, hydraulic elevators, fireplaces in every room, a ballroom, a restaurant, and more turrets, porches, and balconies than all the boardinghouses in Asheville combined, each designed and constructed in the prevailing Victorian style. For nearly forty years afterward the Battery Park Hotel served as the social hub for Asheville society and the destination for its first famous guests, including President Theodore Roosevelt.

40

Soon after the hotel's grand opening, a young George Washington Vanderbilt II stepped off his family's private train car on the Southern Railway, escorting his mother, the recently widowed Mrs. William Henry Vanderbilt. Newspaper reports labeled her the richest woman in the country, thanks to her husband's shrewd investments and renowned collection of railroads. In 1887, mother and son travelled to Asheville so that Mrs. Vanderbilt might convalesce in the mountain air. Her doctors had mistaken chronic exhaustion, a typical Manhattan malady among the wealthy socialite class, for an early stage of tuberculosis. She and her youngest son stayed for several weeks in the Battery Park Hotel, where their suite of rooms provided George Vanderbilt with panoramic views each morning of the mist laying low in the French Broad River valley to the south.

While his mother recuperated on the arm of Dr. Westrey Battle, Asheville's most dapper and charming physician, George Vanderbilt explored the French Broad River valley on horseback. Before the Vanderbilts returned to New York, twenty-five-year-old George, his recent $6 million inheritance (the equivalent of more than $150 million today) burning a hole in his pocket, hired a local attorney to quietly begin buying all the land from the Swannanoa River to Mount Pisgah, twenty-five miles away.

By the time George Vanderbilt returned to Asheville with the venerable architect Richard Morris Hunt in tow, he was Asheville's largest landowner, holding deeds to nearly 125,000 acres of land stretching from what is now known as Biltmore Village to the peak of Mount Pisgah. The sixty-three-year-old Hunt had served as the Vanderbilt family architect for decades, designing palaces and mansions for them along Manhattan's Fifth Avenue and on the coast of Newport, Rhode Island. But young Vanderbilt gave him the opportunity to ensure his immortality by creating not just the finest of the Vanderbilt mansions, but the largest home in all of the United States.

From their horse-drawn buggy, Vanderbilt and Hunt selected a site on the rounded bluff overlooking the French Broad River, three miles from the entrance to the property, and sketched out a path for the winding road that would guide guests through the heavily shaded forest and along the lazy Swannanoa River before emerging into the brilliant sunshine a hundred yards in front of a palace that would be the envy of any European monarch.

Vanderbilt's army of workers toiled for five years on his home after completing the first stage of the project: constructing a railroad line to the site where they unloaded a small mountain of Indiana limestone. Vanderbilt and Hunt, far more accustomed to the accommodations afforded them in Manhattan rather than the more modest offerings of rural Buncombe County, soon retreated, assigning the task of managing the mass of men, materials, and daily details to Richard Sharp Smith, a young Englishman from Hunt's architectural offices. And while it would seem that George Vanderbilt's greatest contribution to Asheville would be the Biltmore Estate, those who have walked the streets of Biltmore Village, the Montford historic district, Albemarle Park, and downtown Asheville may well have taken more delight in the scores of homes and public buildings designed by Richard Sharp Smith.

Undoubtedly shocked by the prospect of leaving New York City and living for the next five years in an old farmhouse near the site of the planned Biltmore House, Richard Sharp Smith packed his bags, stepped aboard the Asheville-bound Southern Railway, and never looked back. While Vanderbilt and Hunt scoured Europe for the finest antiquities, sending back crates of gilded furniture, old masters' oil paintings, tapestries, and sculptures, Smith stood amid the dust and thunder, Hunt's drawings in hand, making sure that no detail was omitted, no change made without his approval.

After five years, however, Vanderbilt's patience with the slow pace of the construction began to grow thin. In the summer of 1895, as Hunt lay on his deathbed, Vanderbilt pulled Smith aside and announced that he was moving in that fall and would be hosting a Christmas party for the entire Vanderbilt clan. Any rooms that were not completed by then were to be sealed off.

With Biltmore House completed, Richard Sharp Smith unleashed his creative powers on a new project: Vanderbilt hired him to design a number of houses on and near the estate, as well as the Young Men's Institute and Biltmore Village, since converted into a collection of shops, galleries, and restaurants. Before the village was completed, George Vanderbilt brought his bride, Edith, home to the Biltmore Estate. Smith was suddenly dismissed and was replaced by the son of his former boss, Richard Morris Hunt. The younger Hunt's commissions left virtually no imprint on Asheville. However, Richard Sharp Smith stayed in the area and enjoyed a prolific and creative twenty-five-year career that no Asheville architect before or since has equaled.

Smith's arrival in Asheville coincided with that of another man who would have a lasting impact on the city's architectural fabric. Edwin Wiley Grove, like others of that era, hoped to escape the rigors of business—in his case, running his St. Louis-based enterprise, the Paris Medicine Company—by escaping to Asheville, where he built a summer home on a knoll in north Asheville. The multimillionaire had made his fortune with his trademark Grove's Tasteless Chill Tonic, an effective remedy for malaria, provided it was taken twice a day nearly year round.

By age fifty Grove had tired of the daily grind of running a major business, so turned his attention to real estate investments and developments, acquiring land in Texas, Arkansas, West Virginia, Georgia, Florida, and North Carolina. Always alert to his next opportunity, Grove began buying rolling pastures and mountainside property on the north side of Asheville until he had accumulated nearly 1,200 acres by the turn of the century. But unlike George Vanderbilt, Grove was not seeking to isolate himself in a palatial estate. He divided much of his land along Kimberly Avenue into narrow lots on streets he named after his wife, children, and relatives: Gertrude, Evelyn, Katherine, and Edwin. He donated three acres at the end of the streetcar line on Charlotte Street for a city park named, coincidentally, the E.W. Grove Park. The donation came with one caveat: Grove could erect a fieldstone office in one corner for his latest business, the Grove Real Estate Company.

When sales of his residential building lots sagged during a major recession in 1908, Grove began to seriously consider a plea from Asheville officials to build a modern hotel to replace the aging downtown Battery Park Hotel. He soon enlisted the help of his talented son-in-law, Frederick Loring Seely, who was ready to leave the newspaper the two men had founded in Atlanta. As with their earlier endeavors, Grove provided the materials (in this case, land) and finances while Seely handled the design, implementation, and management.

Where the Battery Park Hotel had represented the ornate Victorian style and the Biltmore House looked as if it had been lifted from the French wine country, Seely selected the more austere Arts & Crafts style for his new hotel, to be called the Grove Park Inn. Its walls were built from boulders brought from Grove's property and laid with mortar carefully kept out of sight. On the rock, moss and lichens were not only left undisturbed but were proudly displayed, as the hotel embodied Frank Lloyd Wright's axiom, "Built of the land, not on the land."

Equipped with every modern feature—an indoor swimming pool, three-lane bowling alley, elevators muffled inside two enormous fireplaces, rooms furnished with Arts & Crafts furniture, a restaurant serving fresh foods and offering advice on healthy eating—the Grove Park Inn opened on July 12, 1913, and was immediately hailed by the international press as "the finest resort hotel in the world." As Grove and Seely had predicted, the Grove Park Inn soon attracted legions of well-heeled visitors, from tired New York businessmen to wealthy retirees from Miami to Washington politicians.

This natural, inviting environment drew people from across the country, many of whom, like Secretary of State William Jennings Bryan, decided to buy one of E.W. Grove's lots near the Grove Park Inn and to hire architect Richard Sharp Smith to design and build a house in the Arts & Crafts style. In the years following the arrival of Colonel Frank Coxe, George Washington Vanderbilt, Richard Sharp Smith, Edwin Wiley Grove, and Frederick Loring Seely, Asheville blossomed, as it embraced a diverse array of various architectural styles in a growing number of charming neighborhood developments.

Between these two architectural masterpieces — the Biltmore House to the south and the Grove Park Inn to the north — visitors today still discover inviting neighborhoods of Arts & Crafts bungalows, stately Georgian mansions, a smattering of Mediterranean villas, modest Cape Cod cottages, and refined Queen Anne residences. These neighborhoods are punctuated by a half dozen Art Deco public buildings, designed by architect Douglas Ellington and sited haphazardly around the downtown during the heady days of the Roaring Twenties, when Asheville officials and real estate moguls believed that the city's allure and real estate bubble could never burst.

Together these landmarks and neighborhoods weave a rich, if irregular and sometimes irreverent, fabric of architectural styles. The mixture of styles sets the tone and provides the backdrop and the character for a city that is at once historic, trendy, comfortable, and funky. And, most important, a city that is respected and preserved by those who have come to call it home.

---

BRUCE E. JOHNSON is an historian who writes regularly on Asheville, the Grove Park Inn, and the Arts & Crafts movement. He received the Thomas Wolfe Memorial Literary Award in 2009 for his book *Grove Park Inn Arts & Crafts Furniture*. His most recent books include *Tales of the Grove Park Inn, Arts & Crafts Shopmarks*, and his novel, *An Unexpected Guest*.

# Chicken Hill, 1943

HOLLY IGLESIAS

Happy days came and went, as did the songs that Roy Price and his wife sang as they walked to the mill and back. Until the crash, until the strike that left five men dead beside the fence, until she expired birthing the girl. Two babies on his hands and nothing but a quilt to keep him company till Lillie came along, right out of the blue. How she soothed him, that woman, cooing at him, pulling lint from his hair, bearing him three more sons, all swiftly baptized by pressing their heels into a bowl of dough. Biscuits with beans, biscuits with corn: Heaven was made of this, Roy knew it, and his five children in bleached flour-sack shirts knew it too.

**HOLLY IGLESIAS** is the author of *Angles of Approach, Souvenirs of a Shrunken World, Hands-on Saints,* and *Boxing Inside the Box: Women's Prose Poetry.* She has received fellowships from the National Endowment for the Arts, the North Carolina Arts Council, the Edward Albee Foundation, and the Massachusetts Cultural Council. She teaches in the Master of Liberal Arts Program at the University of North Carolina–Asheville.

# McCormick Field

*"What a ballpark! What a beautiful place to play!"*
— Babe Ruth, 1931

MICHAEL McFEE

**1.**

I watch the old man keeping score
a few rows down, a few seats south
here at the new McCormick Field,
each pitch, each out, each hit, each run
recorded in those blue boxes
whose empty frames his hand will fill,
a system my late father tried
to teach me forty years ago
in the original ballpark
when he sat by me marking up
another Asheville Tourists game.
The old man licks his pencil's point
the way my dad would always do.
He doesn't eat, he doesn't drink:
he watches closely, then he writes
until each at-bat's finally done,
part of a neatly-tallied sum.

**2.**

Up narrow Biltmore Avenue toward the park,
up the faulty sidewalk from the after-hours lot,
up the gray stone stairs, footworn as a cathedral's,
up (in dad's hands) to the barred ticket window,

up the concourse crowded with hunger and thirst,
up the section ramp, a loud cramped tunnel,
up the steep concrete steps to our own two seats:

fold down, sit down, look down on the field
glowing before us like an immaculate garden.

3.

For years, my father-treasurer kept the books
for the postal credit union, spreading out
those wide black ledgers on our kitchen table,
each page a grid of pale red and blue ink
ready to be filled with columns of numbers,
additions, subtractions, subtotals, balances.
He'd pencil figures and then punch them
on the massive Remington Rand machine,
pulling its cocked arm for noisy hours
to see if his accounting had worked.
It's no wonder he loved to keep score,
to enter and update and save all the data,
each player's position assigned a digit
from 1 to 9, pitcher to right fielder,
each play a letter or abbreviated cluster:
BB, HBP, DP, 1B, SB, PH, RBI, K.

I was far too impatient to practice
the shorthand dad used those summer nights.
But he'd still let me mark his scorebook
when one of our Tourists went deep
and I got to write HR, then draw four lines
to connect the dots of the bases,
then color the infield solid with my pencil
until it shone, a soft black diamond.

4.

The field was named for Dr. McCormick,
Asheville's first resident bacteriologist,
who was so appalled by the plague of flies
swarming the livery stables and streets
that he started a campaign in 1904:

"Swat That Fly!" It began with local kids
paid by homeowners to kill *Musca domestica*
as it paused rubbing its filthy legs together,
then spread quickly across the country,
a grassroots public health success

that earned him a nickname: "The Fly Man."
And so every batter who swats another fly
and every fielder who runs to haul it in
continues that extermination mission
begun a century ago right here in town.

5.

We'd find the best view of home plate
under the grandstand roof, behind the screen,
so his scorebook wouldn't get wet
and we wouldn't be blindsided by line drives

and we could watch the pitches break
or sink or rise or hiss past the batter
trying to protect the strike zone,
that phantom pane of glass, that grave in air,

as the ump's fingers sprouted strikes
on the right hand and balls on the left, outs
clenched with a fist, his fingertips
resting lightly on the catcher's shoulder
as he leaned forward, waiting for
the next approaching blur he had to call.

Dad said the only better seats
were in the press box perched up on the roof,
that heaven right above our heads

where writers and announcers watched the game
and quickly turned it into words.

6.

Thomas Wolfe was a tall batboy
for the Skylanders in 1915,
loping toward home
to fetch the cast-off lumber.
"Hurry up!" the manager yelled.

Tom loved how the plate
was simple as a kid's drawing,
a single-gable white house
every hitter wanted to get back to.
"Son," the catcher growled, "move it."

7.

We went so often, father and son,
our programs' lucky numbers won stuff:
a case of Royal Crown Cola
whose heavy beveled bottles clinked
all the way to our trunk,
whose wooden crate we never did return,
twenty-four square holes
in which I displayed all the balls I'd collected;
free oil changes, dry cleaning, burgers;

and (most exotic of all) a string tie,
a bolo made in San Antonio,
its slide a flat red baseball
with white feather stitches and TOURISTS
pressed into the sharp-edged plastic.
*Why did they reverse the colors?*
I wondered while sliding that bloody circle
up and down the dark blue cords,
the metal-tip aglets clicking as I walked.

8.

The old man sharpens his pencil
with a pearl-handle pocket knife
like the one dad used to carry,
cedary shavings at his feet
like peanut shells crushed under mine.

9.

The fireworks started early
one Fourth of July:
my nose exploded in a sudden bleed,
my father quickly stanching it
with his handkerchief and surprising pressure,
jamming a piece of folded paper
up under my top lip
and making me lie down across his lap,
head hanging back into the aisle,
legs stretched out across a couple of strangers
who never stopped watching the players.

And dad never stopped scoring them,
my chest his desk
as I studied the rafters and the light standards,
the sparrows bearing scraps of food
and the swooping bullbats clearing the buggy air.

10.

Heilman in right is a blur, kicking weeds:
thanks to a couple of green pitchers
who won't even make the team,
his Detroit Tigers are losing 18-14
to the hometown Asheville Skylanders

52

in their brand-new park's official debut—
wooden grandstands packed to capacity,
low rail fences lined with dark-suited men
tilting their black hats forward
to keep the cold sun out of their eyes.

April 3, 1924, not a single leaf on a tree
in this black-and-white panoramic photo,
not an ad in sight, the only sign
a motto crowning the roof: ASHEVILLE —
THE PLAYGROUND OF AMERICA.

53

Cobb, the bitter Peach, player-manager,
fumes in center with hands on hips;
Manush waits in left for this exhibition
to be over, it doesn't count for anything.
.403, .358, .334: that's what they hit last year

but still finished second to the Yanks.
One day these three will be in Cooperstown,
bronze plaques shining from the Hall's walls,
far away from the leather-lung hillbillies
whose grass they water with major-league spit.

11.

"Great game, Magoo, too bad
you can't see it!"
I lacked the guts and lungs
to insult the umpires,
every ticket-holder's right
my father once told me.

"How can you sleep
  with all these lights on, blue?"
All around us, red-faced men
  would cup hands around mouths
  and megaphone abuse
  on those crooked judges,
  their heckling sometimes echoing
  off the encircling hill:
"Hey ump, the eye doc called,
  he's fixed your glasses!"

"*Asses,*"
  came the longed-for after-jeer.


12.

Later in '24, the Skylanders
(too many letters to stitch across a chest?)
were quietly rechristened the Tourists,
acknowledging the many summer visitors
to The Playground of America

but also the players, coaches, and umps
who hoped they were merely touring Asheville,
sojourners soon to be in the majors,
not on their way down and out of pro ball
or stuck in this mountain-girt town for good.

13.

The scoreboard flashes H, not E:
the old man shakes his silver head.
A home-field ruling, undeserved,
but he erases and corrects
then adds an asterisk and note,
his unofficial marking-down.


14.

Dad knew all the ballpark regulars —

the blind black guy who watched each pitch
loudly on his transistor radio,
always a second or two behind the action,

the retired band director Mr. Denardo,
pained by the bad canned music
but beaming in his box as he conducted us,
holding the ascending notes of "old . . . ball . . . game"
till everybody collapsed, laughing,

Struttin' Bud Shaney, star pitcher
for the '28 Tourists, best team ever dad said,
later the crafty groundskeeper
who could sculpt and pack and water the basepath
so it favored the Tourists that night
or hindered the visiting Phillies or Braves —

and they knew him, another local
who'd played the sport well once upon a time
and prayed for a son and got lucky
and brought the boy here when he was a tiny baby
and ever since so that he could learn baseball
by simply being inside it,
a language they shared without speaking

as they sat side by side, night after night,
never closer.

15.

The Bambino died in Asheville:
that was the rumor in April of '25
when the Yankees trained into town
and Babe fainted in the stucco depot
in front of a mob of star-struck fans

and was rushed off in an ambulance
and didn't leave town with the team
after they won at McCormick Field.
The *Citizen* reported he had "the flu"
but the evening *Times* ran a picture

of the Sultan of Swat flat in bed,
hands folded helpless on his big chest,
which helped fuel the wildfire gossip
that "the flu" really meant he was dead,
a victim of his unchecked appetites,

struck down in the blue mountains
celebrated for their healthfulness . . .
Six years later, Ruth and the Yanks
were back, he and Gehrig homering
high over the steep right-field bank

into the crowd that couldn't get seats.
*I wish I'd asked my dad if he was there.*
This time, the over-the-fold photo
showed Babe winking at the camera
as he kissed a cute young V. A. nurse.

16.

The mound's a low mountain
on the mowed plain of the field,
an ancient volcano
erupting strikes through Dock Ellis
and visitors like Nolan Ryan,

but I was 12 in the summer of '66
so I loved offense and Bob Robertson,
our moody slugger with a swing
so compactly fierce
that when he caught one on the sweet spot
his bat rang the night like a tuning fork,
that deep sound thrilling our seats' wood
and my startled heart
and my rising father's tingling palms
and the trees beyond the left-field fence
waiting for his towering blow
to finish its re-entry in leafy darkness.

17.

"Take . . . me out to the ball . . . game,"
we stood and sang, seventh-inning stretching,
the only time my old man and I
ever lifted up our voices together in song.

"Buy me some peanuts and cracker jack,"
the kids would shout, and the drunks
would lift their last beers and laugh
and toast "I don't care if I never get back!"
as we shared our true national anthem —

not the unsingable "O-oh-say can you see"
crackling overhead before the first pitch,
a few fans mouthing its baffling lines faintly,

my dad's hat over his heart, his smiling lips still,
both of us waiting to cry "Play ball!"

18.

Just north of the park was Valley Street,
the "Niggertown" where nervous whites
taking a shortcut to First Baptist
told their kids to lock the car doors
against idle Sunday morning porchsitters.

Back in the forties, black fans could stroll
down the long hill and fill McCormick
to cheer for their Asheville Blues,
playing Negro Southern League games there
whenever the Tourists were on the road.

I never saw Colored fountains or bleachers
but as I root-root-rooted for Willie Stargell
the air around me shifted uneasily.
Now Valley Street is a brief cul-de-sac
ending behind the county courthouse and jail.

19.

Dad wrote his proud surname in the lead-off spot
the summer I was a Babe Ruth All-Star shortstop
and we played one afternoon at McCormick Field.
I ran from the dugout in my Sealtest Dairy uniform
(leaping the fresh basepath lime) to the very spot
where Davey Concepcion had starred the previous year,
then warmed up with the South Buncombe infielders

before removing my red cap and facing dead center,
watching the star-spangled banner too hot to wave
as I tried to calm the butterflies by praying hard
*God, please don't let the ball be hit my way, please*

and it wasn't, I fielded no chances in two innings
and struck out in my one at-bat, but no matter,
I'd played on the field where my heroes had played
though no picture survives to prove I ever did
and dad's record vanished with all his scorebooks.

20.

He marks the Tourists as he marks
the Sand Gnats, River Dogs, Catfish.
I wonder: does he save those sheets,
or does he keep such faithful score
for its own sake, for the pleasure
of noting every lit movement
for a few hours, for a few months,
for who knows how many decades?
—A crisp objective pencil stroke:
three outs, another inning done.
The old man flips his book and waits.

21.

In college, I swore off sports as bourgeois
though my father still asked me to join him
at the park, when the Tourists were in town,
or in the den, watching cable baseball
the way we once watched the Game of the Week,
laughing at Dizzy Dean's corny malaprops,

but I said No thanks, and so he sat alone
with the close-ups and the instant replays,
falling asleep as Atlanta lost again.


22.

The last time I saw the original park
was in a New York theater, summer of 1988,
a cameo in *Bull Durham*:

Asheville skyline in the background,
Crash Davis drives his Mustang convertible
up the hill, past the stone staircase,
through the right field gate and out of sight.

McCormick was then the oldest baseball field
in the minors, fifth oldest in America
after Wrigley, Fenway, Tiger and Yankee Stadiums —
a dank antique, cramped and dim and haunted,
like the national pastime.

Three years later, they razed its rickety wood
for a concrete and brick "neo-traditional facility."

23.

My dad and I study Ted Williams
finishing his sweet lethal swing,
torso twisted but balanced
between bent right leg stepping forward
and left leg dipping slightly at the knee
so that back foot lifts on its ball
as it pulverizes the dirt,
front arm parallel to swung bat
lifted clean and flat over his shoulders.

We stand side by side, looking up
at this painted basswood statue
of the Splendid Splinter homering,
father and son sharing baseball again,
making their long-delayed pilgrimage
to the Hall of Fame in Cooperstown.
Dad cocks his head and turns my way
and I expect him to appreciate
the finer mechanics of hitting
as demonstrated by the follow-through
of his favorite batter of all time —
No. 9, The Thumper, The Kid,
dark keen eyes lifted, still on the ball —
but instead he asks a question
that stuns me into disbelieving silence,
this white-haired ancient touching my arm:
"Now, just who is that, son?"

24.

May 27, 2004: it's Thirsty Thursday
at the new park, rebuilt on the original site,
and dollar-beer attempts to start the Wave
keep collapsing before it can undulate
all the way around to the bleachers,
and Ted-E Tourist, the bear-like mascot,
is dancing lewdly on the home dugout roof,
and the lesbian couples stand to cheer
when the enormous P.A. voice booms,
after some inter-inning mock Sumo wrestling,
ATTENTION: NO SMOKING IN THE STANDS,

but the old scribe ignores it all,
updating numbers until the next batter steps in.

25.

I don't know how the afterlife unfolds,
but on that cold March day my father died
at St. Joseph's, a couple of blocks south
of the original McCormick Field,
spring training scores already brightening
the hospital TV above his bed,
I hope he made it to that beautiful place,
the doomed ballpark that Ruth himself admired,
and lingered in the shady stands a while.

I hope he made his way out to the infield
then climbed the unraked mound, that circle of dirt
he'd focused on for almost seventy years,
and peered back in toward home, a ghostly zone,
waiting for the dark-blue-suited figure
to gesture that the game could now begin,
waiting for his catcher to give the sign
(one index finger pointed toward the ground
where his body would vanish in a few days,
under the outfield where nobody plays),
waiting for his teammates' scattered chatter
and whistles to pierce the wide air behind him
before he started his delivery,
the first of many pitches in the nightcap.

26.

He stays until the final out,
records it calmly, 5 to 3,
then closes the cardboard covers
and slips the sharpened pencil snug
inside the metal ring binding.
Wincing, the old man rises stiff,
picks up cushion and umbrella,
passes me on the sticky steps
and disappears into the crowd
high-fiving tonight's victory,
the scorebook tucked under his arm,
a clear accounting of the game

that could be read by anyone
(a fan, player, sportswriter, coach)
who understands his steady marks
and loves the always-shifting stats,
the unforgiving truth they tell.

27.

It's beautiful the way this bright field fills
a lofty little valley between hills,

how perfectly they cup the outfield arc
with viny banks and trees, a natural park

or amphitheater for the timeless play
we watch to end another summer day.

---

**MICHAEL McFEE** has published fourteen books. The most recent, *That Was Oasis* (Carnegie Mellon University Press), is his eighth full-length collection of poetry, and concludes with "McCormick Field." An Asheville native, he has taught in the Creative Writing Program at University of North Carolina at Chapel Hill for several decades.

# Altamont Always

DALE NEAL

BEFORE I KNEW ASHEVILLE, I knew Altamont. Before I found my home for most of my adult life, I knew my place from the writer who wrote *You Can't Go Home Again.*

I'm talking of course about Thomas Wolfe, the writer of legend, but of little talk these days among critics or most readers. Before Asheville became my hometown, Wolfe had memorized its streets, the surrounding ring of mountains, the train tracks, and, of course, the people who would turn into immortal characters in his fiction.

I came to Asheville to work at the *Asheville Citizen-Times,* the same daily newspaper that Wolfe delivered as a young boy in the poorer neighborhoods of the mountain town. If Wolfe could rise from such beginnings in the back end of North Carolina, perhaps I could write my way home as well.

My first copy of *Look Homeward, Angel* came under a Christmas tree when I was fifteen, perhaps the perfect age to read his first novel. I still have the paperback—a stone, a leaf, a door on its cover. Opening the book was like walking through that door and stumbling upon what Wolfe called "the buried life." Here was someone talking about what it felt like to be fifteen and alive and alone in all the strangeness of America.

But I am not alone. Generations of readers have had that experience, including such writers as Pat Conroy, Kurt Vonnegut, Cynthia Ozick, William Gay—all of whom have cited their adolescent allegiance to Asheville's most famous son.

In his time, Wolfe rubbed shoulders with Faulkner and Fitzgerald and Hemingway, the pride of American novelists. In recent years, he's fallen from favor, kicked out of the canon of American literature, rarely mentioned in writing workshops at universities and colleges. In bookstores, readers are more likely to ask for books by the dapper New Journalist–turned–novelist Tom Wolfe than by Thomas Wolfe.

The rap against Wolfe has been that his books were the creations of his editors—first, Maxwell Perkins who edited *Look Homeward, Angel* and its sequel *Of Time and the River,* and then Edward Aswell, who culled two posthumously published novels, *The Web and the Rock* and *You Can't Go Home Again,* from the massive manuscript Wolfe left at his untimely death in 1938.

The centennial of his birth in 2000 saw the release of *O Lost,* the original manuscript that would be edited into *Look Homeward, Angel.* A worshipper of all things Wolfe, I went back to reread the even longer manuscript. Matthew Bruccoli and his wife, Arlyn, carefully restored 66,000 words in 147 passages cut by Perkins to give readers Wolfe's original vision, a shapely saga of the soul, an ambitious novel not only about one lonely boy growing up in Asheville, but about America itself growing up as a nation.

The Bruccolis restored the lengthy opening scene, more than fifty pages that Perkins trimmed about the early life of Oliver Gant, Eugene's larger-than-life father. As a boy, Gant witnessed the epic battle of Gettysburg that changed the course of the Civil War and American history. He also encountered the strange mountaineer Bacchus Pentland among the Rebel troops, a foreshadowing of the family he would later marry into at the end of his wanderings.

Wolfe elaborated a whole history for Gant from his apprenticeship as a stonemason in Baltimore to short-lived respectability in Raleigh. Gant was married twice before his wanderings brought him to the far hills of Altamont and Julia Pentland, his third and final wife. Eugene, Wolfe's alter ego and hero, won't enter the book until page 60.

In *O Lost,* Wolfe used the real names of his family he would both immortalize and excoriate. We see his penny-pinching mother Julia, his martyred sister Mabel, his felonious brother Frank, and the stuttering Fred of the crazy laugh.

*O Lost* reminds the reader of that long-ago infatuation with Wolfe's heartfelt rhetoric, offering scenes that still blow you away with the chill mountain winds of Altamont, and others that, well, seem only overblown.

Perkins trimmed away Wolfe's sexier scenes, willing to push the envelope only so far for the mores of 1929. He also red-lined some satirical scenes that show Wolfe's sharp eye and almost drunken love of language, as well as raucous asides about the inhabitants of Altamont. These passages show the young writer's debt to James Joyce and *Ulysses.* Wolfe aimed to do for Asheville what Joyce did for Dublin, jam all of life and emotion and feeling into an ongoing novel.

But as I read Wolfe in his hometown, I saw that he had a keen eye as well as a poetic touch.  He perfectly described how the wind blows up Walnut Street on a blustery winter day in Asheville, how the pebble-dash stucco layers the old large houses in Montford, how the mountains begin to blaze with color and the air turns crisp as a Granny Smith apple come October.

Wolfe left large shoes to fill for any would-be follower. Literally, his supersized oxfords have been bronzed outside the Thomas Wolfe Memorial site, the original Dixieland boardinghouse he immortalized in his novels.

Asheville nearly lost that landmark and a piece of its soul when an arsonist torched the memorial in 1998. After five years of painstaking work, the house was lovingly restored to its heyday at the turn of a previous century. Wolfe's boyhood home still draws visitors from around the world.

On the house tours—still only a buck per adult and a half dollar for kids—the crowds still hush when ushered into the upstairs room where Ben, the older brother, died in reality and again in Wolfe's re-imagining.

But for all his understanding of adolescent angst, Wolfe is more than a teenager's first real writer. He champions the outsider, exposing the heartache of all captive souls who know a larger, richer world exists beyond the narrow confines of their small town, their maddeningly middle-class family.

The British writer Doris Lessing once said of Wolfe, "He did not write about adolescence; to read him is to re-experience adolescence. . . . I have yet to meet a person born to any kind of Establishment who understood Wolfe, I have yet to meet a provincial who has cracked open a big city who does not acknowledge that Wolfe expressed his own struggle for escape into larger experience."

But Wolfe's genius wasn't just to flee Asheville forever, but to forever return to it, to the Altamont of his imagination. Eugene dreamed of faraway cities like Corinth and Byzantium, and Wolfe himself would tramp through Brooklyn, London, and Berlin, but both the fictional alter ego and the living author would discover that the realities of childhood experience are as exotic as any foreign capital. In a real sense, you can't go home again, because you never truly left that place inside you, but it can take years and many journeys to make that discovery for yourself.

All of Wolfe, but especially *Look Homeward, Angel*, makes us remember our first readings, our first encounters with literature that can change our lives. All I know is that Asheville is a place where terrible angels walk among us, and among the archangels who forever sing their aching hymns is one named Wolfe.

---

**DALE NEAL** is the author of the novel *Cow Across America*, winner of the 2009 Novello Literary Prize. His short fiction and essays have appeared in *Arts & Letters*, *Carolina Quarterly*, *Marlboro Review*, *Crescent Review*, and many other literary journals. He works as a journalist for the *Asheville Citizen-Times* and lives in Asheville with his wife and dogs.

# Sensing Boundaries

# Hallowed Ground

DANIEL PIERCE

"IF ANY REAL RACE FANS were offended by my comments, I am truly sorry, but all the tree-huggers and queers can still go to hell." These words, spoken by Asheville stock car racer Ed Surrett, constitute both one of the strangest public apologies and one of the most unusual victory lane celebrations in recorded history. At the same time, Surrett's sentiments reflect a historical divide in the Asheville community between those with deep ancestral roots in the area and those who are relatively recent arrivals. No incident better illustrates that tension than the closing of the Asheville Motor Speedway (AMS) in 1999, which prompted Surrett's decidedly un-politically correct comments.

AMS was built in 1960 on the site of a former dirt airfield in West Asheville. The track soon became a centerpiece of the largely white, blue-collar, Southern Appalachian community. The roar of race cars and the cheers of fans on Friday nights became as much a part of the sensory experience in the community as the taste of cherry cokes at the Ideal Drug Store, the smells of something being fried at the Tastee Diner, the feeling of hair down your shirt after a haircut at the Model Barber Shop, or the sounds of evangelical preaching up and down Haywood Road.

The track could be a rough place, with hard-drinking fans (and competitors) and frequent fistfights that broke out over rough racing on the track and occasionally in the stands. Yet, the track was also a family place, and regulars knew where to sit to avoid most of the trouble, claiming their seats in the stands much as regular church-attenders might claim their spot in the pews. Indeed, for many, the speedway was like church with its pre-race prayer, the passing of race helmets for collections to aid community members in need, and its own variation on communion rites where beer was substituted for wine and white bread (in this case wrapped around a hotdog or piece of fried bologna) for the unleavened host.

74

The locals' attachment to the racetrack was most vividly illustrated by the funeral of James Carver in May 1999. Knowing that he would soon die from a long-endured heart condition, Carver made an interesting request of his family. "I want to be brought around the track. Promise me when I die, you'll have them take me around." Many of Carver's fondest memories during his fifty-two-year lifetime were from the Asheville Motor Speedway. He never missed a race. As *Asheville Citizen-Times* columnist Susan Reinhardt observed: "He followed the races as if they were his calling."

When Carver died, family members convinced speedway and funeral home officials to honor his last request. Family and friends gathered in the grandstands and stood as a car bearing checkered flags on each side pulled onto the track. A black hearse carrying the body of James Carver's remains followed, a stock car with its throaty roar providing appropriate accompaniment to the scene brought up the rear of the procession. Carver's daughter Lisa yelled out, "Daddy, I love you." One sister commented, "At least he got to do it"; while another observed, "He's happy now. I bet he's smiling, too."

By the 1990s, however, for many of Asheville's recent arrivals, the speedway represented an irritation rather than a sacred site. Asheville had changed dramatically, with a large influx of individuals moving to the area from places — physically, socially, and psychically — where stock car racing was not akin to a religious experience. The city, with its beautiful surroundings, healthful environment, and quaint local culture, had long attracted well-heeled outsiders. In the 1980s and '90s, Asheville — and its increasingly funky, Art Deco downtown — drew an eclectic mix of aging former hippies, new agers, arts and crafters, gays and lesbians, and retirees who came to stay.

As newcomers filled the downtown area, West Asheville, with its cheaper real estate prices, attracted many of the younger arrivals. The community that had once taken pride in the speedway began to take on a new face. The greasy diners, gas stations, pool halls, and evangelical churches favored by working-class locals were replaced with funky consignment shops, organic groceries and bakeries, coffee shops, and trendy restaurants. Haywood Road, the central avenue of the neighborhood, now featured the Rainbow Mountain Children's School ("a national leader in alternative, holistic, and contemplative education") and the Organic Mechanic, as former West Asheville anchors such as Fortune's Hardware and May's Market closed their doors.

At the same time as newcomers flocked to Asheville and the city began to develop a worldwide reputation for its cultural, artistic, and culinary offerings, life for many locals began to decline. The real estate boom caused housing prices and property taxes to rise. A new political class, composed almost entirely of recent arrivals, began to control local politics and favored extensive investments in public arts, parks and greenways, public festivals promoting the city's diversity, and attractive signage and lighting in downtown. While these improvements attracted more outsiders, they cost much more in tax money, further alienating locals.

To make matters worse, by the 1980s and '90s, the industrial base, which had been the lifeblood for many local families, was in rapid decline. Thousands of jobs at American Enka, Sayles Bleachery, Ball Glass Manufacturing, Gerber Foods, and Beacon Blankets vanished overnight. While jobs in construction, real estate, health care, and the service industries helped take their place, they generally lacked the stability and benefits of industrial work. This also meant that for many families, children would have to seek their fortune elsewhere. For close-knit families who went back many generations in the region, this fact delivered a psychic and spiritual blow.

The changes created a distinct cultural divide in the community, with many locals not particularly happy about the culture and values that had arrived on their doorstep and many newcomers not especially thrilled with the cultural conservatism of their new neighbors. This conflict was often played out with bumper-sticker wars that immediately declared whether the driver was a local or a newcomer. *We Still Pray* bumper stickers (prompted by a federal court decision to ban prayers at public school football games) were answered by *We Still Read* stickers; Christian fish were countered with fish with legs emblazoned with *Darwin. John 3:16* battled with *Coexist.*

In 1998, the tensions between locals and newcomers came to a head over the Asheville Motor Speedway. While the noise from the speedway was music to the ears of many locals, the Friday night races were a nuisance to new West Asheville residents, and indeed to many across the French Broad River who could hear the roar of the stock cars as well. The presence of the track on the river and its environmental impact also bumped up against the increasingly influential vision of environmental and community development activists who dreamed of a riverfront lined with parks and greenways rather than warehouses, sand drags, junkyards, and racetracks.

The seeds of AMS's destruction were sown in the late 1980s and early 1990s. First, the arrival of activist Karen Cragnolin to the community brought an energetic and determined leader to the effort to reshape the French Broad River area. RiverLink, the nonprofit agency she organized, soon became a major player in local community planning and in the politics that shaped it.

Secondly, in 1993, local accountant Roger Gregg purchased the speedway. Unlike previous owners, Gregg had no real interest in auto racing—indeed, he had never been to a stock car race before he became the speedway's owner—but saw the approximately $1 million he paid for the property as an investment. Whether he cared anything for racing, the historic track, or the people who frequented it, he soon became embroiled in the day-to-day operations, including dealing with the frequent complaints from neighbors about the noise emanating from the track on Friday nights and increasingly assertive city officials who demanded Gregg do something about it.

By 1997, Gregg was openly shopping the track to prospective buyers, although most observers (including the drivers and fans at AMS) assumed any potential customers would be interested in continuing the racing at the nearly forty-year-old facility.

Quietly, however, Gregg had opened negotiations about selling the track to RiverLink which would, in turn, donate the property to the City of Asheville for a park. By the summer of 1997, the two had settled on a price of $1.1 million, and Cragnolin started seeking donations to fund the purchase. She applied for a grant from the North Carolina Clean Water Trust Fund (on whose board she served) to purchase the property. While the trust fund only approved a $250,000 grant (Cragnolin recused herself from that vote), it gave RiverLink the leverage it needed to seek further donations.

In May 1998, while Gregg opened the track for the season, RiverLink signed a six-month purchase option on the property. No one in the racing community had any idea that the end of auto racing at the speedway might be near, because all these transactions were held in secrecy; even discussions with city council and other city officials were held in closed executive session. By early fall, Cragnolin had received commitments from other donors—two major private foundations and two large donors who wished to remain anonymous.

After the racing season ended, details of the confidential deal were ironed out, and a resolution to accept RiverLink's donation was prepared for the October city council meeting. Included in the AMS deed transfer was a clause stipulating that if the city accepted the donation of the property, auto racing would be forever banned at the speedway. Near the end of the council meeting, with no public notice, the council voted unanimously to accept RiverLink's donation and its terms. There was no public discussion of the issue, and council members gave Cragnolin and Gregg a standing ovation.

The news spread rapidly through the local racing community with most fans and drivers blaming an Asheville elite who cared little for working-class pleasures. Local NASCAR legend Jack Ingram — who began his career at AMS — spoke for many speedway supporters when he told the *Asheville Citizen-Times,* "It's a small minority depriving us. It's definitely political. I believe there should be a big protest march and I'll lead it if possible." City council members were flooded with irate phone calls, and the *Citizen-Times* featured front-page articles almost every day for the next few weeks laying out details of the deal and quoting angry fans and drivers.

Gregg and Cragnolin jumped to their own defense. "I was not guided in this transaction by my own monetary interests," Gregg claimed. "I was guided by what I perceived as the best interest of the community." He also said that owning the racetrack consumed a lot of time that he would prefer to spend with his sixteen-year-old son. "You only have one chance to spend time with your family," Cragnolin asserted. "We're not against racing. This was an opportunity. A wonderful opportunity."

The more the two talked, the more they were perceived as elitists, out of touch with local culture and the mourning of the local racing community. To many, Cragnolin seemed oblivious to the impact of the loss of the historic speedway to locals. She spoke of the land that could now be used for greenways and soccer fields and that the old speedway itself was "a wonderful place for a concert."

Gregg grew increasingly testy in his comments to reporters. When asked what he thought about the memories of race fans, he responded, "The memories of the owner are radically different from the memories of the fans." As for the drivers, "There are many places they can race." The most dramatic confirmation for many locals that this was just another example of the contempt many in positions of power held for them came when Gregg averred, "This is not a great business financially. And it certainly is not a great business culturally."

The behind-the-scenes role of the Biltmore Company, whose famous estate lay just across the French Broad River from the track, also came to light. Shortly after the announcement of RiverLink's donation, a Biltmore spokesperson admitted to the press that Biltmore was the source of one of the anonymous donations. She quickly denied any connection between the donation and the announcement the previous month that the company was constructing a $31 million dollar luxury hotel a half mile from the Asheville Motor Speedway site.

An editorial in the *Asheville Citizen-Times* succinctly wrapped up the situation for many locals.

> City council members who have fielded calls from West Asheville residents disturbed by the noise from the racetrack, RiverLink officials whose goal is to clean up the river and provide parks and green space along it, and the donors who support that end all thought this was a great win-win situation. No one seems to have given much thought to the thousands of racing fans.

City council members did seek some redemption by negotiating a deal where fans and drivers could have one final season at AMS in 1999. "Final Thunder," as it was billed, was a melancholy experience and a long, sad goodbye often characterized by tirades from victory lane like that issued by Ed Surrett.

The season culminated in the final race at the speedway on September 17. Sportswriter Keith Jarrett wrote an eloquent epitaph for the place and for its significance to locals in that day's *Citizen-Times*:

The closing of **AMS** is about thousands of members of an extended family that meet every Friday night from early April to early September, gathering at their second home for sport and competition, for recreation and relaxation, for fun and for usually very little money. . . . The thought occurs that those responsible for the shutdown of **AMS** are perhaps in need of a little time in front of a mirror and for more than one type of reflection while asking the question — Would you want your family treated like this? But the answer isn't really important, because 40 years of racing at **AMS** was never about them.

After the speedway closed, the controversy began to die down. RiverLink and the city procured funds to turn the track into a first-class park complete with basketball and volleyball courts, a huge wooden playground, outdoor roller-hockey facility, a lawn bowling court, and picnic shelter. Use of the racetrack itself was limited to bikers, runners, and walkers, and the peloton replaced the packs of growling stock cars. Asheville Motor Speedway was renamed Carrier Park in honor of the airfield that once claimed the site.

For many years there was no indication of what had gone on there most Friday nights for forty years. In 2007, City Councilman Jan Davis initiated a movement to construct a memorial to racing at the park. He raised support from the city and county, private donations from **AMS** fans, and, ironically, a sizeable donation from the Janirve Foundation, one of the principle donors to the RiverLink purchase. The six by eight foot, checkered-flag memorial was dedicated in September 2010 with several hundred race fans and most of the members of the city council in attendance. The dedicatory plaque expressed the feelings of many of those gathered there that day:

Today, the asphalt oval remains, incorporated into the park as a bicycle track. Bicyclists pass the scuffs and dents on the outside wall left by four-wheeled machines. And perhaps without knowing it, they are sharing the lanes with the ghosts of powerful race cars, driven by men who became legends and others who just tried. For those who know and believe, this is hallowed ground.

Probably few Asheville residents who use the park to play roller hockey or basketball, lawn bowl, or ride their bike consider this ground *hallowed*. For the few remaining locals who do, however, the track and the memorial stand as a shrine to an Asheville that once was, but has long since vanished.

---

**DANIEL PIERCE** is the author of *Real NASCAR: White Lightning, Red Clay, and Big Bill France* and *The Great Smokies*. His work has been published in the *New York Times, Southern Cultures, New Encyclopedia of Southern Culture,* and other publications. He has been featured on programs, including NPR's "Talk of the Nation" and the History Channel. He is professor of history and resident professional cracker at the University of North Carolina–Asheville.

# A Tale of Two Cities

JOHNNIE GRANT

*Like any child, I lived in a world full of curiosities. It was a childhood confused by the complexities of a life that made it so different, restrictive, and guarded. Different by the invisible boundaries I didn't understand. Restricted and guarded by the watchful eyes of the adults in my life whose vigilance was filled with half-truths of kind words intended to protect my heart from what was yet to come.*

AS A YOUNG STUDENT attending St. Anthony's Catholic School (an all-black private school managed by the Franciscan nuns), I lived a regimented and disciplined life. School days were filled with English, math, history, social studies, etiquette, catechism, and French—with little time for recess. It was an education taught to the sobering taps of yellow chalk on a blackboard, and to the threat of a chastening rod that kept the students attentive. By fourth grade, St. Anthony's students were fluent in French and instantly could respond to a dialogue of conversational French initiated by the instructors. It was a level of discipline that met the approval of parents who sent their children there to learn.

When spring came, students looked forward to the school days giving way to much-needed summer vacation, a time for freedom and explorations. Five of my friends and I would plot our quest for each summer day. We took our planning sessions seriously; after all, vacation *was* our exception to all rules, and we intended to fill it with as much fun and excitement as we could.

With the curious innocence of many young children, I managed to escape the watchful eyes of babysitters and persuade my play-partners to explore different parts of Asheville. Our adventures took us through the uptown corridors of Eagle and Market streets (the black business district fondly known as the Block), and down neighboring side streets and alleys looking for anything that might interest our curiosities. We awed at the beautiful ornate buildings and the bustling uptown businesses. Our journeys took us through the halls and staircases of the Del Cardo, Ritz, Wilson, and other buildings in the business district. There were barbershops, beauty shops, attorney and dentist offices, restaurants, tailor shops, and even a billiard hall to which we were denied entry.

We nestled in obscure places, watching life unfold before our eyes. The adults who became familiar with our charades gladly bought us treats to keep us out of mischief. One of our biggest feats (after much persuasion) was landing counter-stool seats at the YMI Drugstore soda fountain. We feasted on some of the best hotdogs in town (compliments of the older patrons), washed down with a tasty, thirst-quenching cherry coke. The counter stools allowed us a picturesque view of the activities outside the panoramic glass windows. We stared in fascination at people bustling from shop to shop and giggled at overindulgent customers being escorted from nearby restaurants or bars to the sidewalk. We watch in amusement as they danced down the street to whatever tune was playing in their heads. For us it was living life out loud, and we were amused by the carefree spirits of those people!

After a day of exploring, we would make our way to the woods of Beaucatcher Mountain to strategize about our next expedition. On the way home through the East End community, we would be reprimanded by the elders who were responsible for keeping watchful eyes on all the neighborhood children.

Each adventure took us farther and farther away from the familiar. Eventually, we landed in unfamiliar territory—downtown. As I looked around, my instincts told me to turn around, but my curiosity kept me moving forward. The awe of it all was overwhelming.

Looking around Vance Monument we noticed two water fountains nearby. Being a hot day, a cold drink of water would be just the treat. As we lined up at the fountain waiting our turn, we began to attract the stares of white men and women.

Near the fountains were steps leading under the monument plaza. Lots of people disappeared downstairs. Being so inquisitive, I had to find out what was down there. We noticed a policeman across the street, so if any life-threatening incident occurred we were sure that he would come to our aid.

We cautiously crept down the steps knowing one false move could lead to our demise. As the morning sunlight gave way to darkness I could hear my friends whispering, begging to turn back. "No, we're at the bottom!" I said and reached for a door handle. As I touched it, a person inside pushed the door open and began yelling at us with a thunderous voice. Paralyzed with horror, we stood there looking at the giant, our backs against the wall. I could feel splatters of pee hitting the lower part of my legs and realized I'd just wet my pants. Farther up the line of my friends, I heard water hitting the cement stairs, letting me know I wasn't the only person who had peed her pants. We were shaking like wind-blown leaves.

"You're not white—you're colored—I'm going to have all your asses thrown in jail—git the hell up them stairs right now, and git away from here—you don't belong down here!" He continued to scream at us, while pee ran down our legs. Ignoring our accidents, he marched us up the stairs like captured soldiers. Being at the back of the line, I heard the man laugh as he kept his diatribe flowing.

People had gathered in front of the Vance Monument to see what the confusion was about. They gasped as our captor moved us onto the plaza. We were all just as wet as we could be! People began to laugh. The man lit a cigar and rocked back and forth making claim to his prized catch. "See what I found downstairs?" he said. While the crowd grew, he motioned for the policeman, who frantically blew his whistle and waved his police club, creating another spectacle along the street as drivers slammed on their brakes.

Suddenly, the man pulled something from inside his suit jacket pocket. My friend almost collapsed, fearing that he was pulling out a weapon. But it was a Bible. "We gonna have to do something with these coloreds!" he began. "This is an abomination before God, and we can't allow this to happen in Asheville." He pointed to the places where we should or shouldn't be. He preached fire and brimstone for approximately twenty minutes (a lifetime for us), relating every admonishing word to scripture. We stood there — like prisoners of war destined for the guillotine — while the man preached what we thought might be the last words we would ever hear.

Standing there in shock and embarrassment, we witnessed the white audience clap in agreement. One of the man's words resonated in my mind — *colored?* Who is *colored* I thought? I didn't dare open my mouth to ask for fear of being beaten down by the policeman's nightstick.

Finally, by some divine intervention, the man let us go. We took off running fast as our legs would carry us! We didn't stop running until we arrived back in familiar territory. The warm weather had partially dried our clothing, but the urine stains were visible. The adults reprimanded us, saying we shouldn't play to the extent we would pee on ourselves. Little did they know what we had just encountered.

As summer turned to fall, we gathered in the woods to learn from each other what it meant to be *colored*. We began reading books, newspapers, and magazines, anything to understand why this man called us what he did. I never had been call *colored* before, and I had never been talked to in that manner. Above and beyond that, I just couldn't get the word *colored* out of my mind. I thought *colored* meant colors of rainbows, crayons I used to color in coloring books!

We began to learn that being colored meant barriers and limitations; barriers that dictated where we could travel, eat, shop, live, learn, play, and worship. We learned that one of the water fountains we drank from was designated, "Whites Only," as were the bathrooms under the Vance Monument—we had gone in the wrong door. We began to learn the lessons of oppression, and what that oppression could do to the psyche of African Americans who lived through Asheville's de jure racial segregation and urban renewal, which razed more than 425 acres of family homes and businesses, the after-effects of which are still felt today.

The history of African Americans in Asheville is not esoteric. It is a tale of survival, resilience, perseverance, sustenance, and beating the odds.

Yes, life is a learning process that is filled with uncharted territories.

Being so inquisitive on that summer day long ago, I had to find out what was down those steps, where I discovered a world I wasn't quite ready for.

---

Asheville native **JOHNNIE GRANT** is the publisher of *Urban News*, a local multicultural community publication. Her view is an excerpt from her forthcoming book, *The Place of My Chagrin: Movement I.*

# What You Seek Is Seeking You

GLENIS REDMOND

SITTING ON A WROUGHT-IRON BENCH at the intersection of Walnut and Lexington streets, catty-cornered to Carolina Lane, I was waiting for the slam to begin at the Green Door, a local music club that hosted the Asheville Poetry Slam. My Type A personality had me there geek-early, two hours before, in order not to miss one moment. Perched on the bench, no one would have guessed how far I had traveled to get there. It was even farther than the seventy-five miles or so I just had driven from Simpsonville, South Carolina.

There were so many worlds that I had to rise out of in order to plant myself on that bench in that particular city in that particular moment. I was amazed at how the universe had to contort me in such a way that I had to perform a spiritual Houdini in my life to get where I needed to be and to pay attention to what my heart had been murmuring all along. I finally listened.

A few hours earlier, I left my office at the Care Center, where I worked as a clinical counselor, and headed up the mountain. Once in Asheville, I slipped into the basement bathroom of the Pack Memorial Library, ditched my professional wear, and changed into a more casual *poetic* look: jeans, boots, and a free-flowing cream top—my hair already braided. I was ready to be washed and revived in the word.

It was almost an hour and a half before the slam began, so I walked a few doors down and entered Malaprop's Bookstore. I had been introduced to Malaprop's before I ever set foot in Asheville. A year earlier, the bookstore had set up a table at the Healthy Connections Conference in Greenville, sponsored by the agency for which I worked. The conference was timely; it took place at a point in my life when I was very ill and had just been diagnosed with a chronic illness: fibromyalgia. In true book-aholic fashion, I bought six books at the Malaprop's table and told my friend Dabney Mahanes not to let me purchase another one. She failed, because yet another book kept calling my name— *The Artist's Way,* by Julia Cameron— I bought it too.

Synchronistically, Dabney called me the next day and told me that there was going to be an Artist's Way workshop; I immediately signed up for the twelve-week workshop with twenty-one other people. It was there that I discovered poetry again, and at the end of the course, I began to believe that I might be a poet and I just might have something to say.

I could not voice it then, but looking back, Malaprop's Bookstore acted as an oracle in my life. When I entered the old Malaprop's, in its former glorious cramped space, it seemed to know what my soul was pondering; and in response to my internal questions, books seem to fall off the shelf into my hands. Obviously I needed *The Essential Rumi,* because it landed in my palms and I purchased it. I had just been introduced to Rumi through Bill Moyers's PBS series, "The Language of Life." In it, poet Coleman Barks recited Rumi to music and it made my heart bloom. One of my favorite Rumi quotes spoke to me in that stage of my life:

> Today like every other day we open up empty and frightened. Don't open up the door to the study and begin reading. Take down a musical instrument. Let the beauty we love be what we do.

The beauty of poetry emboldened me and I began to follow. Asheville was the place on the map where I could flower. Where it was taking me, I did not ask. I just knew I was becoming more alive. I had begun to put my fears and emptiness down, even though my doctor had handed me a grim prognosis. He said, "You're not gonna die, but you'll sure wish that you had."

Poetry diverted my gaze from muscle pain, interstitial cystitis (ulcers on the bladder), and an endless amount of food allergies. What fueled me most were my passions, the two P's: Parenting and Poetry. I would come to learn how one passion fed the other. That is how I found myself on the bench downtown that day, reading poetry, waiting on more poetry.

Out of the blue, an older black man appeared and sat down beside me. His skin was a deep, rich mahogany and he was over six feet tall. His face was not quite withered, but was lined in such a way that gave him character and made him seem timeless. He stood out too, because not many blacks graced downtown. He had a scar that ran down the right side of his face, as if he had been in a knife fight. His presence and visage were both arresting and alarming. Head burrowed in my book, I was visibly ignoring him, but the poet in me noted everything about him. I did my best to throw off nonverbal cues that radiated, *Leave me alone.*

He did not take the hint; he began to talk. *The Essential Rumi* that I intently read was no defense. He even asked me what I was reading, trying to penetrate my self-erected force field. In my best off-putting manner, I answered, "Rumi, a thirteenth-century Sufi mystic poet," hoping this reference to the arcane would make me stoic and impenetrable.

His response was, "What's your sign?" My inner self was doing all kinds of eye rolls—the thought-bubble over my head would have read, "I give you Rumi and you give me some broke-down line about my sign, brotha please." In actuality, I said, "Virgo."

After this not-very-friendly comment, he turned into some kind of street-roving gypsy, spouting his own brand of astrology and philosophy. He told me that Virgos were more practical and normally did not tend toward the arcane. He said that I must be on the cusp. That's when I gave him The Look: my glasses tilted just a little, so I could peer over them with that no-nonsense gaze.

He kept right on talking and walking a tightrope between the worlds of trying to pick me up and trying to educate me on Asheville's history. When he tried one of his over-used lines, a fire engine whizzed by blaring its alarm. He said, "Okay," to no one in particular. Then he announced, his voice intense and booming, "I'm angry at Asheville." This explosive anger came out of nowhere, like he had.

His mood bordered on rage. I was ready to exit. This was not a safe place.

"I am angry at Asheville, because it ignores Black Asheville." I settled down a little when I heard the phrase Black Asheville. I listened, because I'd grown up starved for my own South Carolina history that was not taught in high school or college.

He spun his tale, telling me about the alliance between the early Cherokee and African Americans, and how the blacks taught the Cherokee how to build wagon wheels and the Cherokee taught blacks how to navigate the land. He talked about how you never hear that the two co-existed and had built a profitable trade, transporting goods and people through the mountains until the railroad was built, destroying the commerce of this alliance.

He said, "Asheville needs to do better with telling our story." He had given me a lot to hold on to. In poetry I was beginning to unearth my own lineage and here he was passing on stories that I needed to hear, learn, think about, and write. This stranger on the bench was scattering knowledge, and as an African American poet, I collected it.

Then he made another smarmy remark, trying once again to pick me up. As soon as he did, another fire engine passed, as if on cue. He looked up again to the sky and said to the air, "Okay, I get the message."

I got the message, too. Uncanny. I felt my worlds within worlds merging—as if Rumi had reached his long poetic arm from the beyond. His words, "What you seek is seeking you," resonated. Poetry was seeking me out in a way that talked to my authentic self. I never saw the man again, but I wondered about our timely meeting. There is a Buddhist proverb that says, "When the student is ready the teacher will appear."

Later, when I moved to Asheville, my poetic gaze turned toward the direction in which the man on the corner of Lexington and Walnut had pointed me. It was not a conscious decision, but my pen was following my heart. I needed to write about those who had walked the land, their voices never heard. The slave cemetery near my home in the Kenilworth neighborhood became an obsession of mine.

My poet's gaze also turned to a little-known history—a band of freed slaves that lived outside of Flat Rock, in a placed they had dubbed the Kingdom of Happy Land. After being emancipated in the 1860s, they walked from Mississippi to Flat Rock, starting out as a ragtag band of twenty-five and ending up with more than a hundred seeking a place to live peacefully. They worked for a Civil War widow, mining the land and crafting herbs. They made balms and salves for the farmers and laborers.

The stranger who sat next to me on the bench that day, like the poetry of Rumi, pointed a way in which I needed to travel. It was not until I slipped free from the bondage of silence that I could speak/write about what was in my heart.

I left the bench and the stranger, and walked down Carolina Lane to the Green Door, my head full of the lessons of Rumi and of Asheville from long ago. I knew unequivocally that I was where I needed to be; too many signs had led me in the direction toward Asheville, toward my own growth.

The Green Door that day and many others provided a space for me to develop tools and skills that would further strengthen my own poetic voice. It deepened my social circle. I befriended people—Bob Falls, Allan Wolf, Christine Lassiter, and others—who would walk alongside me as they traveled their own poetic path. I kept stepping out into the greater world, telling my story, giving voice to my ancestors' stories. Poetry allows me to express another view, one that in my opinion expands the landscape with a complicated beauty.

## Footnotes

Where does history go
when it hasn't been tended?
I say it grows wild amongst the Periwinkle,
the Turkey-foot fern and my mind.
There it is right alongside my heavy heart
like that mass of stones left on a hill
the only remnants left of the Kingdom
speaking of mountain royalty,
King Robert and Queen Louella
leased for ten cents a day
by a Civil War widow, named Serpta.
Their rule over 200 acres of chopping,
hauling and toting.
I understand this urgency,
the need for self-appointment.
I hear it in the restless wind on the ridge
or are those ancestral voices crying out
about the uneasy quilt-stitch hearsay
of their lives being left to myth and lore?
Where does history go when it dies?
When corn cribs and makeshift houses
no longer riddle the mountain slopes
and forty years of hands culling Comfrey
into a healing balm. Where Gospel Songs cease.
This silent edge is where I live
filled with heartache remembering history
and where it goes without a foothold.

## Storm Warning

The roads in my heart lead to a place
that won't let the past die. Sorrow calls
and I waver, a weather vane that reads the signs
like Coosawatchie, Tallahassee, a red road chant.
Close by storms of plantations and field songs brew,
a blood stirred that leaves me bothered and alive.

**GLENIS REDMOND**, a native of Greenville, South Carolina, has lived in North Carolina amongst the Cherokee Mountains for the last fifteen years. A graduate of Erskine College, she earned an MFA in poetry at Warren Wilson College. She is a Cave Canem Fellow and recipient of a literary fellowship from the North Carolina Arts Council. Her latest book of poetry is titled *Under the Sun.* Her website is www.glenisredmond.com.

# Some Gals Are Just
# Not Meant for the Dog Park

I HAVE NO SOCIAL LIFE, so to speak. Being a writer is a lonely job. Being a mother is a full-time job. This leaves precious few moments for friends. I guess that's why somebody invented Facebook. You get to pretend you're popular without leaving the house.

Sometimes, though, adults get lonely and need stimulation from other grown-ups. Book club is great, but only meets once a month. Plus, it's hard for me to always pretend I actually had time to read the book. I think the girls are on to my game.

Then I discovered another way to get out of the house that didn't involve reading or pretending to have read. My fiancé bought me a dog, as if I weren't crazy-busy enough. Buddy, the vivacious Border collie, was actually a gift for my daughter. Of course, after two weeks she got tired of tending the wild one, so his care was pretty much left to me. And Buddy was one hard dog to keep busy.

Not long after receiving this kangaroo-hopping pet, one of the smartest and most energetic breeds ever born, I realized I needed to walk him.

The big snag (and excuse) is that I live on a hill in Fairview. It's hard on this old gal's knees to trudge a wild dog up and down mountains.

That's when I discovered dog parks, the perfect place to sit on your fanny and socialize with other proud pet owners. There's one park on the river off Amboy Road and another off Azalea near the soccer fields behind the WNC Nature Center. The latter became my place of peace. But not for long.

At first, I thought of the dog park the way other people might think of Starbucks—a spot of joy, a multitude of flavors, dogs of every breed and size, but not a mocha chocolate latte in this bunch of various canines. Some people sip Chai tea at coffee shops around town. I plop down with a Diet Coke in the expanse of lovely, smelly mulch.

Oh, but don't get me started on the owners, most of whom are quite nice and have become my "Dog Park" friends. Others are, well, either too boastful or for some reason bring in fang-bearing dogs, their hackles raised and ready.

One can't just go to a dog park and expect to unleash the pooch, sit back, and relax. Believe it or not, there's a certain etiquette expected from both dog and owner.

On my inaugural visit, I didn't know the rules. Buddy, a herding dog bred to tend sheep, decided to pull the collars off every animal in the park. When he grabbed a pitbull's collar, the owner slapped my baby angel and called the po-po on us. I had to go hide near the Nature Center to wait out the blue lights.

Soon, I learned the rules. Be certain your dog is calm and acclimated before taking him off the leash. Dogs in packs can be quite unpredictable. Also carry along a jug of water for all canines, and make sure you've got poop bags aplenty. Owners get awfully mad when a dog squats, does his thing, and no one rushes to the scene with a wrinkled old Ingles bag to sweep away the offenses.

Owners also love to brag. There's more boasting in a dog park than a preschool where uber-moms talk about their kids mastering calculus at age four.

Dog-park bragging is different. I call it the Reverse Brag. It goes like this:

"Oh, what an absolutely adorable dog," I say to a lady sitting next to me
on one of the benches.

"Yes, she's the best dog on the entire planet. We rescued her from
a puppy mill where she weighed only ten pounds and was one hour away
from being put to sleep."

Or this:

"Pokey is such a calm and cool dog. We rescued her from a shelter in
Boone where they already had an IV in her ready for death. We came
in at the exact right moment."

All the owners like to carry on and on about their rescue dogs.
Which is great. And which leaves me feeling flushed and burning with the
embarrassment of owning a purebred. I try to explain that Buddy came
from a very poor farmer who had to sell the dog to feed his family of fourteen. This is a lie. I'm sorry, Lord.

The owners also like to talk about a dog's grooming and hygiene. This
also leaves me hot-faced. My dog likes to swim in sludge, and every time
he leaves the groomer, he's filthy in forty-five minutes.

The other day my friend Joan, a precious doggy owner, commented
on Buddy. "We didn't recognize him," she said in her effervescent voice,
her rescue mix by her side. "He's soooooo clean."

What could I say? I didn't want to tell more lies. "I guess all this
rain washed him off," I said. Then I couldn't resist. "He has an appoint-
ment with the groomer next week." Lie. Lie. Lie.  I vowed to go home
and brush his matted haunches, maybe take a bit of liver toothpaste to
his fangs.

At least next time we hit the park, he'll smile as if he's been wearing Crest White Strips.

One of my dearest friends has a dog like mine — wild, smart, and high-maintenance.

Last winter, after multiple snows and harrowing surgery, I had neglected my wonderful Buddy. My friend Nancy, too, felt her dog, Hercules, needed a mini-vacation. So we decided to introduce the dogs. Hercules, a boisterous, lurching lab, and my herding dog, Buddy, played rough as two fullbacks on a corn-fed football team.

We were delighted they got on so well. The next step was getting up the nerve to take them to the dog park where I still remained on the "Most Wanted" list since the earlier pit-bull incident and other breaches in dog-park etiquette. Besides, people would just see bronco-style galloping Buddy coming and cringe or make snide comments. "There she is with that dog of hers," a roughneck with another pit bull said. "He better stay away from my Sugar Bear."

Sugar Bear, by the way, is a pit bull that's not nice. When this puff-jawed dog's around, I try all I can to keep Buddy at bay.

It was a lovely afternoon when Nancy and I took our dogs to the park and let them loose. They caused instant chaos, as if tigers had suddenly been set lose in the park. People just don't understand the "active" ADHD dog demeanor of some breeds. They may have little Chihuahua mixes that run around like battery-operated toys or laid-back labs that do nothing more harmful than fetch sticks on command.

We sat on a urine-soaked bench and watched the action unfold. Let me reiterate: The owners are often more of a problem than their pooches. They will swat your dog, push it to the ground, scold it, all the while turning a blind eye to the destruction being wrought by their dog. Just like school. They act like parents whose kids can do no wrong.

But on that particular day, the air was laced with something weird, something besides the scent of dog. A thoroughly pierced woman roamed the park, methodically checking under the tails of all dogs that came into the larger area. "Mama," my daughter said, "this weirdo came up to me and asked if Buddy was neutered."

I watched this Ms. Hiney Checker poking her head between all the dogs' legs and heard her asking the same question. Finally, I just couldn't stand it.

"Why are you asking if all the dogs are neutered? Do you have a female in heat?"

She scowled and I withered.

"No, I have a male dog that's been neutered."

"Well then, what's the worry? He can't get pregnant, now, can he?"

Uh-oh. Nancy shot me a look. I was very close to being tossed out of the dog park for a second time. The Hiney woman put her hands on her hips and we squared off.

"No, my dog can't get pregnant, you moron. He just doesn't like male dogs that haven't been neutered."

And maybe you don't like male men who haven't been neutered either, I dared but didn't say.

She left me alone and continued to cruise the park and check all incoming dog butts. My friend and I watched and died laughing.

"I think I'm about ready to go home," Nancy said. "Next time why don't we do this in the little park in my neighborhood. It'll be just Hercules and Buddy. No butt checks."

Sounded good to me. I'm about *over* the dog park dramas.

---

SUSAN REINHARDT is the mother of two and has written four books, including *Not Tonight Honey: Wait 'Til I'm a Size Six*, now in its seventh printing. Her humor book, *Don't Sleep with a Bubba*, was named *January Magazine*'s Book of the Year. She loves to hike with her dog, having given up dog parks, and to impersonate Sarah Palin. She is a columnist for the *Asheville Citizen-Times*.

# A Circle with No End

RICHARD CHESS

Called east.

When you live in Asheville, in Western North Carolina, often you find yourself called east. To take a daughter or son to a soccer tournament in Greensboro or Fayetteville; to attend a professional meeting in Raleigh; to visit a freshman at Carolina; to deliver a surfer to East Coast swells.

Then comes the return trip, west on I-40, much of the ride dull until the mountains come into view, until Old Fort where the ascent toward home begins. In overdrive, the car muscles its way uphill, following the sinuous line of the road, hugging now the outside, now the inside of one's lane. The first landmark: the Eastern Continental Divide, 2,786 feet above sea level.

Then, almost immediately after dropping down into a valley, the second landmark comes into view: the gateway to Buncombe County, a cross towering into the sky from atop a ridge. It's the site of the Lifeway Ridgecrest Conference Center, a place to which, says its website, "ministers and missionaries have been called" and where "thousands have been saved and godly relationships have been formed."

But to me the cross says, *Your language isn't spoken here; you're not wanted here.* What else is new? Welcome home.

Once, I counted: how many churches on my daily route from home to my son's preschool and from there to work? This was in the spring of 1997. My family and I (wife, two stepdaughters, son) had just returned from two months in Israel.

I was on sabbatical. Oops! UNC–Asheville doesn't call it "sabbatical." Today it's called "professional development leave." At the time it was called "off-campus scholarly assignment." Whose language is this? The same creature who says "resident alien," "pre-owned vehicle," "collateral damage"?

One of the first Friday nights of that trip, we had an invitation for Shabbat dinner. Before dinner, we went to a Shabbat service.

On the way to synagogue, I noticed men and women, boys and girls, all dressed for Shabbat, walking in what seemed to me to be every possible direction. Of course: in Jerusalem one can find a synagogue in any direction one turns!

Though I was a mere visitor and a stranger in Kiryat Shmuel, the neighborhood in West Jerusalem where we were renting an apartment, I felt a deep bond to all those who were striding smartly, dutifully on the streets that night, each of us drawn by that hour to his or her choice of a modest or beautifully appointed sanctuary to sing the Sabbath Bride home. Indeed, welcome home.

Seven weeks later, behind the wheel of my old Subaru, my son strapped into his car seat behind me, heading down Beaverdam Road, then south on Merrimon Avenue, I counted: Beaverdam Baptist Church, Parish of St. Eugene, Asbury Memorial United Methodist Church, Grace Episcopal Church, Grace Covenant Presbyterian Church, Merrimon Avenue Baptist Church, Covenant Reformed Presbyterian Church. Five miles, seven churches. No synagogues.

Though I had never counted before, I'd seen these churches, at least in my peripheral vision, more or less daily since I had moved to Asheville in 1989. Now I wondered: Did my son, who had just celebrated his fourth birthday with our Israeli neighbors, notice the churches everywhere as I drove him to and from Shalom, the Jewish Community Center preschool he attended? And if so, what did they say to him?

Signs and symbols. And bumper stickers: *We Still Pray.*

Fall of 2000. ("Fall": having grown up in South Jersey, fall in my life-before-Asheville began the day after Labor Day, the first day of school; here in Asheville, "fall" begins around mid-August, the first day of school.) Suddenly, *We Still Pray* bumper stickers, slapped on the bumpers of every 4x4, minivan, and sedan, were idling at every red light, cruising down every avenue, and parked in every lot in Buncombe County.

Launched by a few pastors in Asheville in response to a U.S. Supreme Court ruling that found that student-led prayers before high school football games violated the principle of church-state separation, the We Still Pray movement was formed to encourage outbreaks of "spontaneous prayer" in public high school stadiums before the Friday night football games.

That fall, my family spent Friday nights the way we spent most Friday nights of the year: gathered with friends at one of our homes for potluck Shabbat dinners, complete with blessings over candles and kids, wine and bread. The last place I wanted to be was in a high school football stadium, not even to observe firsthand what the rest of the country was then reading about in their newspapers and magazines. Including in *The New Yorker.*

"God and Football: The Fight to Keep Prayer in the Stadium," by Mark Singer, posted from Asheville, appeared in the September 25, 2000, issue of *The New Yorker.* "God and Football" begins with two local spiritual leaders responding to a question: How many churches do you think there are in Buncombe County?

"Well, I'm sure we have as many churches as we do restaurants," answered Reverend Buddy Corbin of Calvary Baptist Church. "Bazillions," said Rabbi Robert Ratner, now Rabbi Emeritus of Congregation Beth Ha Tephila. "There are a lot more churches in Asheville than restaurants. And that includes the fast-food places."

Reading this story even now, eleven years after it was published, I'm struck by how profoundly it affects my sense of *my* place in *this* place. *The New Yorker* had been drawn to the epicenter of a movement whose tremors had spread throughout the American South. And in the third sentence of *The New Yorker*'s report to the world about what was happening in the place where I happen to live, Bob Ratner — my colleague and friend, with whom I've participated in and shared many communal and professional experiences — appears, along with one of the two synagogues (the one to which I don't belong!) in Asheville.

*You are here,* the story tells me. The outsider's gaze fixes me in place.

Just a few days before "God and Football" appeared, the great Israeli poet Yehuda Amichai died in Jerusalem.

At my invitation, Amichai had visited Asheville in the early Nineties to participate in a contemporary Jewish writers festival. He opened the festival with a reading in the all-purpose room (gym, bingo hall, theater) of the old Jewish Community Center, a ramshackle two-story house.

To make room for a new, modern facility — better designed and equipped to meet the needs of the growing local Jewish community — that building was to be demolished the day after Amichai's reading.

"Don't do it." Those were the first words Amichai uttered upon taking the stage to begin his reading. "You'll never be able to replace," he said, pointing to the side of the room, "that lovely wooden staircase."

One poem he read that night was "Tourist." To reassure his mostly American-Jewish, Israel-infatuated audience, he prefaced his reading of the poem by saying that it wasn't an anti-tourist poem.

In the first of the two parts of the poem, Amichai describes, in a gently ironic tone, some of the typical things Jewish tourists do when visiting Israel. Part 2, a prose paragraph, describes the speaker's encounter one day with a tour group:

> Once I was sitting on the steps near the gate at David's Citadel and I put down my two heavy baskets beside me. A group of tourists stood there around their guide, and I became their point of reference. "You see that man over there with the baskets? A little to the right of his head there's an arch from the Roman period. A little to the right of his head." "But he's moving, he's moving!" I said to myself: Redemption will come only when they are told, "Do you see that arch over there from the Roman period? It doesn't matter, but near it, a little to the left and then down a bit, there's a man who has just bought fruit and vegetables for his family."

Amichai is one of the coordinates by which I locate myself as poet, Jew, man. When, after learning of his death, I walked into class that Wednesday afternoon, I was disoriented. The map of my relations had been unexpectedly, sadly altered.

I felt the need to bring Amichai's world and work—Amichai's Jerusalem, Amichai's Torah, Amichai's loves and losses—into Karpen Hall, Room 232, into the lives of twenty undergraduates. Few of them had the kind of sensibility necessary to receive the work, to invite the work to settle, even if only for a moment, into their lives. None of them had the cultural, religious, historical experience and knowledge necessary for the work to resonate deeply within them.

The distance between us in that classroom, in a building named for a local Jewish benefactor whom I had been fortunate enough to know and love, on the campus of the university where I have had the good fortune of being given an opportunity to devote my professional life to meaningful work, in Asheville, North Carolina, which by the fall of 2000 was well on its way to becoming known throughout the United States as one of the most desirable places to live, was too great to cross.

I don't remember which of Amichai's poems I read to them that afternoon. I don't remember how, if at all, the students responded to the poems or the news of his loss.

A year later, on 9/12/01, I read Amichai's "The Diameter of the Bomb" to another class.

> The diameter of the bomb was thirty centimeters
> and the diameter of its effective range about seven meters,
> with four dead and eleven wounded.
> And around these, in a larger circle
> of pain and time, two hospitals are scattered
> and one graveyard. But the young woman
> who was buried in the city she came from,
> at a distance of more than a hundred kilometers,
> enlarges the circle considerably,
> and the solitary man mourning her death
> at the distant shores of a country far across the sea
> includes the entire world in the circle.
> And I won't even mention the crying of orphans
> that reaches up to the throne of God and
> beyond, making
> a circle with no end and no God.

Tragically, the students now had a context in which to read Amichai. We sat in a circle and went around that circle, one by one, each of us who felt so inclined sharing something we noticed in the poem. It was stunningly clear on that unique day that the poem opened to them and they opened themselves to it.

My Asheville. Amichai lives here.

Characterizing a world from which gods with all their promises of a better place beyond this one have disappeared, Wallace Stevens says it will be "friendlier" here when the "earth seem[s] all of paradise that we shall know." Stevens, too, lives in my Asheville, adding the coordinates of Hartford, Connecticut, and Key West, Florida, to the map on which you can locate me.

But you won't find me on Google maps or Garmin. Really. Ask the Jewish students who followed those directions a few weeks ago trying to make it to my house, which is actually easy to find, for a Shabbat dinner.

If you must find me, look here: twenty-one miles west of the Ridgecrest cross, which despite its makers' best efforts, reaches only so far into the sky. I live inside the circle of the sky, a circle of "pain and time," protest and prayer, love and fear, their truth and your truth and mine.

I also live *on* a circle, Skyview Circle, where Jerusalem and poetry pass through a stranger who has resided in Asheville for more than two decades now. While my dog sniffs whatever's growing on the side of the road, I look up now and see a sky with no crosses, no synagogues, not a single god. In the sanctuary of a simple sentence I say—(or is it a voice not mine I hear?)—*Welcome. Welcome home.*

**RICHARD CHESS** is too restless to read one book at a time let alone to live in one place for more than twenty years. Yet that's what he's done, having moved to Asheville in 1989 where he still lives. He is the author of three books of poetry, *Tekiah, Chair in the Desert,* and *Third Temple.* His poems have appeared in many publications, including *Best American Spiritual Writing 2005* and *Telling and Remembering: A Century of American Jewish Poetry.* He is a regular contributor to *Good Letters: The* Image *Blog.* He is the Roy Carroll Professor of Honors Arts and Sciences at the University of North Carolina–Asheville.

# A Place Called Home

# City of the Dead

NAN K. CHASE

TWIN BROTHERS LIE BURIED side by side in Asheville under the rock-hard soil of Riverside Cemetery: Grover C. and Ben H. Wolfe, born October 27, 1892. Grover lived to age twelve, and Ben died eight days before his twenty-sixth birthday, on October 19, 1918, a not uncommon mortality rate among a family with eight children that reflected the state of American medicine and hygiene a century ago.

Their younger brother the towering American novelist and playwright Thomas Wolfe wrote about their deaths in his cruelly accurate novel *Look Homeward, Angel,* without changing their names. Thomas Wolfe had been just four years old when Grover died, and so describes his brother's demise from typhoid fever (while the family was visiting the St. Louis World's Fair) in only two pages. But Ben's agonizing bedroom death scene in Asheville, detailed breath by breath and through a final rancorous exchange with his mother, lasts for fifteen densely written pages, soaked with family drama and golden prose, until, at last, Ben "passed instantly, scornful and unafraid, as he had lived, into the shades of death."

Thomas Wolfe followed Ben to the grave two decades later, dead from tuberculosis of the brain at age thirty-seven, and was buried a few feet away, as were his parents, the darkly complex W.O. and Julia Wolfe, and various sisters and brothers and in-laws, the whole family locked in stony silence in the place Wolfe called City of the Dead.

I go there sometimes because it is the most beautiful spot in Asheville: hilly, green, quiet and still, and cooled by a forest of stately old trees. A "healing and concealing grace of fair massed trees," Wolfe wrote. I go there to be alone with Asheville's history.

In truth I go there for deeper reasons, mainly to honor Thomas Wolfe's fanatical literary devotion to truth. It's not that I enjoy reading his works, for they are painful and difficult and slow, and I can understand the rage they caused among Asheville's townspeople when first published in the 1920s and 1930s. But in them I can inhabit twenty-first century Asheville in real life and yet be instantly connected to the city's glorious, glittering, often disturbing, past. Wolfe wasn't just writing stories, he was writing the autobiography of a city, a city in the midst of explosive growth followed by devastating collapse, a process he foretold and despised and in which his own grasping mother played a part.

I live in that city today, walking the same sidewalks he walked, gazing at the same quaint skyscrapers he saw, resting beneath some of the same trees. I know because he told me how it was then, describing with photographic accuracy so many of the streets and houses and businesses at the turn of the twentieth century, exactly as I see them now. But most of all, Wolfe described the same frantic attitude of anticipation and pride, excitement and danger, that swirled, swirls, and will swirl evermore about the streets, intoxicating all who breathe the air.

And, I venture to say it aloud for the first time, I go to Riverside Cemetery because I feel at home in his City of the Dead and find solace there among the graves of so many who died young; it is a place I understand. For I, too, lost a sibling while a youngster. And among all authors, only Wolfe, to my mind, dares to show how large a part of living is dying, even the moment of dying, and how important a strand is death in the fabric of the world, even when folded over and hidden in the seams. He bores into reality with words, sanding and smoothing with their repetition until all that is left is truth. "In that enormous silence, where pain and darkness met, birds were waking," he wrote about the first moments after Ben's death. "It was almost four o'clock in the morning." That is the same instant on the clock I remember so perfectly, so indelibly, when my own sister passed "into the shades of death," also of unstoppable disease, when I was a teen-ager and she was four years old.

Other people go to Riverside Cemetery to see the simple Wolfe gravesites, of course, and maybe for similar reasons. On the one marked TOM they leave mementos: sometimes small stones, sometimes individual flower blossoms, and most recently, pennies laid into every crevice and curve of his name.

111

I think about Thomas Wolfe a little bit every day — can't help it — because my husband and I moved onto his home turf several years back. Wanting to settle in Asheville, we bought a crumbly vacant lot in an old downtown neighborhood and built a house there. The sensation has been like stepping into a folio of storybook illustrations from the past, so completely were parts of nearby Asheville preserved by half a century of economic slumber after the big bank crash of 1930 brought ruin to the city's real estate tycoons and the merchant class in general. We walk past his mother's infamous old boardinghouse — now the centerpiece of a Wolfe visitors' center — when we head to the center of town; we look to the north and see the undulating red tile roof and the castle-like walls of the Grove Park Inn, completed just as Wolfe was becoming a teenager; we look across the street and one block up and see the Manor, a fairy-tale colony of huge shingled "cottages" begun a year before Thomas Wolfe was born, where later he participated in amateur Shakespeare productions on the park-like lawn.

Closer yet to our home, elegant granite curbstones from that early twentieth-century real estate boom line the streets, and even our backyard has yielded up bits of the past. My husband came into the house one day with a tiny, perfectly preserved clear glass bottle he had dug up while turning the garden, no more than an inch-and-a-half high and a half-inch wide, an antique, with the diminutive threads from a missing screw top still intact, unchipped.

What had that little bottle held? Laudanum? Tears?

---

**NAN K. CHASE** has written for the *New York Times, Washington Post, Smithsonian Magazine, Air & Space,* and other national publications. She is the author of *Asheville: A History* and *Eat Your Yard! Edible trees, shrubs, vines, herbs and flowers for your landscape,* and co-author, with Chris McCurry, of *Bark House Style: Sustainable Designs from Nature.* She lives and gardens near downtown Asheville.

# Sabbath Day at McCormick Field

ALLAN WOLF

Some of us have come direct from church,
some of us from yard work,
some from Sunday morning mimosas,
or brunch time Bloody Marys
to this historic, sacred space
to bask in the grace of nostalgia;
here where the revival's invocation
is "Play ball!" Where communion
is a hotdog and a seven-dollar beer.
Where Amen is a hearty bases-loaded "Whoop!"

The seventh inning stretch is our altar call.
Our souls soar above the outfield wall.
It's Sabbath Day at McCormick Field.
And it's more than baseball, after all.

It's more than baseball, after all.
We shout out, "Charge!"
at the organ's urging.
We raise our hands as T-shirts
slingshot overhead. We cheer
Ted E. Tourist as he mugs
and clowns and loses his race
against the Brownie 'round the bases.

Eager-faced little-leaguers wear gloves
in hopes to catch that foul-ball tip,
dropped like a gift from above.

And we who are grown,
we wear our ball gloves too.
A grown man's mitt is invisible
but rest assured, it's there.

Have Faith.

You must be a believer before you can see
how our innocence waits at the end of our arms
on Sabbath Day at McCormick Field.

---

**ALLAN WOLF** is an author and performance poet living in West Asheville. He has hundreds of poems committed to memory and conducts poetry shows and author visits all over the country. His books include *New Found Land, Zane's Trace,* and *Immersed in Verse: An Informative, Slightly Irreverent and Totally Tremendous Guide to Living the Poet's Life.* His latest book is *The Watch That Ends the Night: Voices from the Titanic.*

# Farm to Asheville Table

RICK McDANIEL

THE SUN HAS JUST STARTED peeking over the ridge tops when the first pickup truck pulls into the North Asheville Tailgate Market. More trucks arrive and soon boxes of Silver Queen corn and heirloom tomatoes, harvested at the first light of dawn, are stacked on folding tables alongside golden yellow crookneck squash and plump okra.

One table offers samples of sourwood honey and organic raspberry preserves on homemade bread to tempt the taste buds. Fresh-cut flowers and heirloom roses catch my eye, but the sweet smell of free-range sausage rising from a skillet on a camp stove pulls me in another direction.

You only need two words to sum up the food scene in Asheville: fresh and diverse.

When the Scottish and German settlers came to the Blue Ridge Mountains in the mid-1700s, they lived and practiced what chefs today are determined to recapture—everything tastes better if you grow it locally and naturally, not that the eighteenth century folks had any other option. But our diets have changed dramatically in the last few centuries, and a massive effort is being made to once again grow and eat "local."

Whether it's rainbow trout fresh from the waters that flow from the peak of Cold Mountain or just-harvested organic vegetables grown by a new generation of farmers, Asheville is home to a vibrant farm-to-table movement. The method for getting the trout and lettuces from the field and stream to the table is no longer negotiated and bartered around a potbelly stove in the general store. Instead home cooks and restaurateurs alike rely on local food stores, tailgate markets, and even online networks to find a bounty of locally grown food. And this movement over the last decade has transformed the mountain city into a food lover's destination.

Just as the way we buy our food has changed, so too have the people who grow it. Farmers today tend to be young, business-savvy, and in many cases, armed with college degrees, many from nearby Warren Wilson College. Some are newcomers to farming; some are former Brightleaf tobacco farmers who have turned to growing organic vegetables and fruits. Regardless of their background, they're committed to making Asheville's markets and restaurants the best they can be.

One of the hallmarks of sustainable agriculture is the reintro-duction of heirloom fruits and vegetables. Local orchards once again are producing apples such as the Honey Crisp, a sweet, juicy variety prized for pies, and the Arkansas Black, which extends the harvest into late October. Cherokee Purple tomatoes, with their unique purple color and sweet taste, and Mountain Gold, prized for their unique color and low acid-ity, are some of the tomato varieties that have reappeared on local farms.

It's been a long journey back to reconnecting Asheville area farms with Asheville tables. When the interstate highway system was developed after World War II, fruits and vegetables from California flooded the South, ensuring fresh produce year-round. Unfortunately, their availability came at a price. These new varieties were bred for transportability, not flavor. The heirloom varieties disappeared from the local market. While you could find a beefsteak tomato in a chain grocery store in February, the tough skin and sterile taste were an abomination compared to the sensual glory of a tender, juicy heirloom tomato ripened by the summer sun on a nearby farm.

Today, these varieties, grown locally from heirloom seeds, offer a flavor unmatched by commercially grown produce. You'll find these "new old" fruits and vegetables in scores of Asheville's finest markets and restaurants.

An important part of Asheville's dynamic food scene is our abundance of tailgate markets. From May to November, you'll find them all over town, offering farm-fresh vegetables and fruits, homemade jams, jellies, preserves, sourwood honey, and scratch-made baked goods, many of these organic. Meats and fish are also an important part of the sustainable movement. Local farms offer free-range, organically raised hogs, beef cattle, turkeys, and poultry, as well as sustainably produced fish.

An important part of Asheville's claim to fame is its many locally owned, independent restaurants. Whether you're looking for California fusion, Caribbean, fish tacos, or traditional Southern cooking, Asheville offers a stunning array of restaurants and bistros for a city its size. In the span of a few blocks you'll find French, Italian, Asian, and Mediterranean.

If all this talk about food is making you thirsty, you'll find plenty of things to wash it down. Asheville has been named "Beer City USA" for several years running, thanks to its nearly dozen microbreweries. If you're in the mood for a local pilsner, a porter, or an IPA, you'll find it at almost any local restaurant. Several of the breweries operate tasting rooms, where you can go to sample the beer fresh off the line in convivial little taprooms.

All these things make Asheville one of the most unique food and dining experiences in the United States. Whether you live here or are just visiting, you won't go away hungry.

---

**RICK MCDANIEL** is a food historian and writer who makes his home in Asheville. The author of *An Irresistible History of Southern Food,* he has served as a regional judge for the James Beard Chef and Restaurant Awards and as a consultant to the producers of "Diners, Drive-ins and Dives" and Anthony Bourdain's "No Reservations."

# Burton Street Working Together

DeWayne Barton

On the west side of Asheville between Patton and Haywood
A community holds on, tries to create a sustainable model
Relationship-building between people
What can I say:  Burton Street?
Start with Mrs. Johnson, former president of the community association
She lives in the 2$^{nd}$ house on the right after the chain-link fence
A house made of brick with a nice landscaped yard, thanks to her husband
    Skip, a rock's throw from I-26
Recently crowned 2011 NAACP "Queen for a Day"
Next door — Ms. Conley, a powerhouse
Community history teacher, member of Mt. Carmel Baptist Church —
One of three churches that bring love and prayers to the area
There's Community Baptist Church and
St. Paul Missionary Baptist Church, rest in peace Reverend Young, where
    the Davidsons attend,
Pillars in the community still put in work, teach youth, deliver food

A community trying to heal and celebrate

Ms. Pearlie Mae at the corner of Burton and Downing taking care of all
the alteration needs

If she sees you work too hard, she rewards you with a big slice of cake

There's the Cunninghams who allowed us to clean off part of their land to
plant flowers and label trees as part of an outdoor classroom

They also run Mama's Fastfood, soulfood on Haywood Road going toward
the city

Many others, essential sources for success

The blood of the body, the water to the earth

Remember Autumn—how the myriad trees explode with color

Beauty Peace Release

Leaves that float down to the Earth's surface

A unity of color coming together

Rich in hope with a powerful history

Working together, but not in slow motion

Shorty—jack of all trades, philosopher, comedian, man of action and smiles

Mr. Cotton decided to return home, Oh what a blessing,

To help guide his grandfather's legacy while taking care of his own

His grandfather, E.W. Pearson—businessman, community advocate,
sports team owner, who established Burton Street Community

Martha Jane—much love—she allows us to work her land to grow food

A mural reflected in the background

Brett with the British accent,

The mind behind the recording studio and technology center in the
basement of the community center

Future solar panels on the roof

The Burton Street Center staff: Tameka, Bam, and LaFeion

Six eyes, six ears, three voices

Dominique, the community's right-hand man

The Mays boys, Brandon, Willie Jean, Ann, and all the youth who have
given a hand

John Grant, urban superhero, always a phone call away

Charles Conley, original poet and storyteller of Burton Street

Honor goes to God that helped guide us to this place

My wife, Safi

My mother, Gwen

Queen bees in my life

The Burton Street Community Peace Gardens, Creative Ambitions

Future greenway at Smith Mill Creek where my grandfather once raised
hogs and chickens

Ujima Market, urban farm, garden, and produce

And plenty of outside community partners:

UNCA, Warren Wilson, ADC, and GreenWorks all come to play

Helping to build relationships among people

Working together

---

**DEWAYNE BARTON**, aka **LLOVE**, is a spoken-word poet, photographer, and performance artist. Born in Asheville, he is the author of *Urban Nightmares Silent Screams, Volume 1*. He is cofounder of Green Opportunities, a job-development program that helps prepare young people for "green-collar" jobs. He is president of the Burton Street Community Association.

# Mapping Life in These Hills

JAN SCHOCHET

1.

JUST BEYOND the two native stone posts at the entrance to Riverside Cemetery, Asheville's past reveals itself. The hilly, narrow paved lanes are lined by large granite stones carved with family names, mountain names—Williams, Patton, Proctor, Westall—names that have dominated surrounding peak settlements and the valley town of Asheville for more than two centuries. There are also many ornate Victorian monuments— angels, lambs, scrolls, columns, obelisks, stone trees (the markers of members of the Woodmen of the World fraternal order)—all memorializing some life, some breath of God in these hills.

It's easy to imagine people a century ago spending a customary Sunday afternoon strolling and picnicking in the cemetery—a stone-dotted green overlay sloping down toward the French Broad River that comforts with tall oaks, rolling hillocks, winding paths, bits of ornate ironwork. The setting invites such activity. Yet no one does that any more.

Riverside Cemetery is quiet, except for birdsong and faint whoosh of cars on the nearby highway hidden by a wall of pines.

Around a hill, a hundred yards from Thomas Wolfe's grave and then O. Henry's, is the Jewish section of Riverside, surrounded by tall hollies. There, the Hebrew letters chiseled into small stones from the early 1880s are worn and difficult to decipher. Straight ahead are the big dignified family plot stones. In English. Dating from the early 1900s. Lipinsky, Sternberg, Blomberg. Particular stones are labeled with first and last names. One of them—large, plain, and cut with tall, thin block letters—reads, *A Blomberg. Born in Linkova, Lithuania. 1845.* My great-grandfather, Aaron.

It's a peaceful place, green and lush with just the right proportion of stone to vegetation, a good place to rest. Riverside is filled with scores of my relatives—Unk, my dad's older brother and my favorite by far (and I his); Aunt Lillian; Aunt Dora; and other aunts, uncles, cousins. And now my dad. They were, altogether, staples of holiday celebrations—Passover, Yom Kippur break-the-fast dinner, Thanksgiving, New Year's Day, Sunday dinner—a part of my daily life growing up. A pantheon of personalities, some dull, some exciting, a few eccentric, some hardworking, others not.

I am grounded in this land. Of it, from it, and to it I return.

2.

Great-Grandfather Aaron and Uncle Louis settled in Asheville in 1887, moving from Savannah where their older brother owned a store. Born in Lithuania, they had better prospects for adventure in a new world than those in the old. The train brought them to Asheville during a population boom—the town growing from 2,400 in 1880, when train construction blasted through the mountain, to 12,000 a decade later.

My family established itself in Buncombe County soil. Its roots grew into many of the shops in downtown Asheville in the early twentieth century. Aaron owned a store and relocated it every twenty years. His six children owned clothing stores (of varying quality) from 1900 through the 1970s. His many grandchildren also had stores—clothing, shoes, jewelry. Over the years my entrepreneurial Great-Uncle Louis turned his little building on the northeast corner of Patton and Lexington avenues into at least fifteen different businesses, from a tobacco shop to an arcade to a movie theater.

Aaron and Louis also became founding members of the reform temple in 1891 and the conservative schul in 1896. Their children helped establish the Jewish Community Center in 1930—the smallest town in the U.S. to have one. Memorial plaques in the temple and schul list all my relatives. It was not uncommon for Jewish families to belong to both. Sometimes a husband would belong to one synagogue, the wife another—a Jewish version of a house divided, though far friendlier.

3.

When suburbs sprouted in the Fifties, my parents moved there—a five-minute drive from downtown. But downtown, the destination of my childhood outings and the one in which my ancestors walked, no longer exists. Today's residents and visitors may not realize that art galleries haven't always filled Asheville's buildings. For every building, there's a story—many stories—of its succession of businesses, some successful, some not. A lot of life went on there, long days at work, parents who came home tired to their children each night.

From my family's experience, I learned at an early age that these businesses were not only a way of life but a constant worry. Would their window get broken tonight? Would they sell enough to make payroll? Would a wealthy patron buy their best wares, chosen at the New York market? Would a fire burn it all down? Should they let that slacker new salesperson go?

No matter if it was 1898 or 1958—the characters changed. But the worries remained.

4.

The first store I remember is my parents' shoe store, the Bootery, now the drive-through for the BB&T Building. The front of the Bootery was small, the size of a living room, with a swinging plywood door that looked like a saloon door in a Western that led to a cavernous stockroom in back. In the retail area, shoes were perched on their little shoebox shelves and looked like a flock of birds about to take flight.

I went to the store most days after school and on Saturdays. It was my jumping-off point. From there, I'd tear through downtown. Exploring. Visiting. Discovering my world.

5.

Urban renewal was a misnomer in Asheville. The town was barely urban in the 1960s. And *renewal* wiped out scores of intact neighborhoods for what would become the expressway—I-240. Some now call it urban *removal*. It demolished the Woodfin Street/Oak Street neighborhood, as well as the Valley Street, Asheland Avenue, and McDowell Street neighborhoods.

Some homes targeted for urban renewal were dilapidated. But others— small shingle houses lived in by older folk and solidly blue-collar workers, and bigger houses containing ground floor neighborhood groceries or shops with proprietors living above—needed only a coat of paint. Their demolition deprived the city of hundreds of dwellings for the as-yet-unimagined revival of today's Asheville.

When I drive up Merrimon Avenue, approaching downtown, and come to the corner of Woodfin, I remember the Burroughs mansion. The dark red brick antebellum building—constructed in 1839 by Nicholas Woodfin and later bought by Dr. Burroughs—was the site of the YMCA, an important part of my childhood.

6.

I remember this: I'm a six-year-old riding in the car while my dad drops off my older brother at the Y for a swim lesson. We watch him walk onto the porch with its tall white columns leading to the old mansion, flanked by two large wings.

One time I asked my brother where his swimsuit was and he replied no one wore them. My eyes bugged out at the thought of so much jiggling for all to view. My brother often told tales I never realized were just that: tales. When I asked, "Even Cousin Sigmund?" he solemnly nodded. I was filled with a sense of dread, imagining a seventy-year-old man swimming naked in a pool with other old, and young, men.

In seventh grade, I took guitar lessons upstairs at the Y. In one corner of the capacious upstairs room, my guitar teacher, a 1960s folkie with thick, brown Beatles hair, always stuck his still-burning cigarette into one of his guitar strings. Occasionally he brought the cigarette to his lips, drew hard, and blew perfect smoke rings that wafted toward the high ceiling of the dark wood-trimmed room. Those were the first smoke rings I ever saw.

Fletcher School of Dance held dress rehearsal for their annual recital in that room too. Hundreds of students changed costumes, lined up, performed, and sat around waiting. The smiling Mrs. Fletcher would mill through the groups of young dancers, her hand extended, inviting gum-chewers to deposit gum into it. We all knew the rule: no gum onstage.

That was the YMCA I knew as a kid. Today a square gold-mirrored bank sits there.

7.

The current YMCA (and health department, and hotel and condo complex) is located on the site of an old neighborhood where much of my family once lived. Great-Uncle Louis and his family lived on the corner of Spruce

and Woodfin. My grandmother lived up Spruce a few houses, just north of
Mrs. Wolfe's Old Kentucky Home boardinghouse. Across the street stood
the original reform temple, old and whitewashed. By the time I was born,
the temple was boarded up, but the schul still sat across Woodfin on property that's now the entrance to the expressway. Cousins and Jewish friends
lived nearby. For many years, it was a regular shtetl of the Appalachians.

Asheville today is much changed. But I also see the life that once was —
a lively neighborhood around the corner from a bustling downtown of
purpose, filled with stores of necessity and indulgences too — hardware
stores, department stores, jewelry stores, shoe stores, banks, music stores,
theaters, and bakeries. Five-and-dimes, the cafes, the S&W Cafeteria.
Bookstores, office supply stores, ladies' fancy clothes stores, furriers. Men's
shops and haberdasheries. Dry cleaners, hat blockers, newsstands. Bars,
pool halls, cheap hotels, the farmer's market, discount shoe and clothing
stores. I remember them all.

Streets bustled: people coming and going, carrying shopping bags,
holding hands, going to the movies, laughing with their friends, sighing as
they locked up their shops, skipping down the street when they got hired,
dragging themselves home if they got fired, walking with a lighter step
when times were good, crying on the front porch during disasters, just as
my Great-Uncle Jack did when his store burned in 1924, killing two people
and ultimately sending him into familial and financial ruin.

Some of the people in those old scenes *were* my relatives — jewelers,
drygoods and shoe merchants. I couldn't walk a block before someone
reported my whereabouts to my mother — Woolworth's, or Cosmo's, the
after-school hangout, or E.C. Goldberg's newsstand.

Six-foot-wide Tom's Grill displayed matzah boxes in the window every
year at Passover — it was the quick lunch spot for many Jewish business
owners. Their wives lunched at the S&W with their friends. Friday nights
the stores stayed open late, the sidewalks so crowded that some pedestrians had to walk in the streets. Thursday family night at the S&W was
a ritual: children could watch cartoons in the special kids' room while

the parents joined their friends at four-top tables in the grand Art Deco dining hall.

Life in Asheville then was as vibrant and colorful as life in Asheville now. Maybe more so.

---

**JAN SCHOCHET** is the founder and president of Gentle Thread Marketing (www. gentlethreadmarketing.com), which helps businesses market through stories. This is an excerpt from a memoir-in-progress.

# Views in Fiction  🌿

# Rattlesnakes

WAYNE CALDWELL

YOU DON'T KNOW ME without you have read a book by the name of
*Cataloochee.* That book was made by Mr. Wayne Caldwell, and he told the
truth, mainly. In it I was James Erastus Carter (my family called me Rass,
to my undying embarrassment), a boy of a dozen years, bad scared by
a rattlesnake. It was a good experience, though. A body keeps running
into them.

Later I "made a lawyer," as they say in the mountains. Had been working
in Asheville a year or so when the war took me to North Africa, Italy, and
France. After the war a classmate and I started a law firm. Worked for fifty
years in downtown Asheville, then retired and decided to foist a memoir
upon the world.

Asheville's scale is small enough that one duly diligent person can know
it intimately. It's a city with heart. But, ever since the train came in 1880,
people from "off" have been moving here, which means someone's constantly trying to force their idea of "better" on it.

People like Dr. E.W. Grove, who died about the time I met my first
rattlesnake. After the war his Arcade squatted like a terra cotta toad atop

the nub of Battery Hill (itself landfill for Coxe Avenue). The building had been an enclosed mall, far ahead of its time, until the government requisitioned it during the war. Federal offices remained until this year. (Easy to go to bed with the government, hard to get out.)

Grove had planned to erect a fourteen-story tower atop it, but his death and the Depression killed that. Seems like every time you turn around, though, some similar erection is contemplated.

Our law office occupied the top floor of what old people still called the New Medical Building, at the corner of Market and Walnut. On a clear day I could spy the Cataloochee Divide from my window. March 13, 1980, I poured a cup of coffee, sat at my desk, and looked toward the mountains over a gray, cold Thursday morning. I was sixty-four, and my body remembered every darn year of it. When I saw the headline in the *Citizen*—MID-CITY MALL—I felt about as friendly as the weather. What in hell are they up to now? I wondered.

Now, I admit that Asheville's 1980 downtown was in sad shape. The Asheville Mall had stolen the department stores (only Penney's remained, and it was searching diligently for a suitor). No crowds of shoppers clogged the sidewalks. No respectable citizen would willingly have walked the streets after dark. It wasn't a ghost town—churches, banks, and lawyers (and a Chinese joint known for serving biscuits and gravy as a side with chow mein, perhaps Asheville's first "fusion" restaurant) occupied many spaces—but those who remembered the boom of the Twenties (or the quiet prosperity of the Fifties) were past concerned. Some were desperate.

City council had created AREDC, the Asheville Revitalization and Economic Development Commission (beware both the Ides of March and governmental bodies with long names), to resurrect downtown. They had been encouraging very small businesses, purchasing street furniture and lighting (paying great sums, I noticed, for streetlamps very like the old ones that became landfill for the Crosstown Expressway), and calling for a local downtown historic district. There was an incipient street festival in late July. (Don't get me started on that.) A Canadian with local ties had begun to buy downtown properties not held fast by absentees and trusts. Progress was measurable—we seemed on the right track.

MID-CITY MALL? The article said the AREDC had the day before unveiled plans for a downtown "retail-hotel-office complex," a development requiring a "public-private partnership" between the city and a Philadelphia developer—who needed, incidentally, forty million taxpayer dollars.

I picked up the paper and looked out the window. A shopping mall as a redevelopment project? A block from our office? I knew the routine. Buildings (eighty-five, as it turned out) would be condemned. Bought by a redevelopment authority. Bulldozed. Gone.

Why, I wondered, had they turned 180 degrees? I called the commission chairman, who invited me to his office to examine the map. I didn't stay long, but carried away sizeable anxiety. They were serious. Metes and bounds? From I-240 and Broadway south to College, a jag west to miss the Kress Building, south to Patton, west to Wachovia, north to College, west to Haywood, north to Walnut, east to Rankin, a jagged line to the beginning. (The little gerrymander that took buildings on Patton didn't stay in the plan.) Seventeen acres. Amazing.

Couldn't help but notice that three commissioners owned property in the area. I hadn't smelled such rotten fish since our last urban renewal. Or, for that matter, since the week before, when an entire block of Patton (across the street from the aforementioned gerrymander) was razed, to the perfect surprise of most people who worked downtown.

Shades of Dr. Grove. The Ghost of Christmas Future.

I knew who would support it. Various ex-mayors, bankers, the newspaper, the television and radio stations, the chamber of commerce, the merchants' association, some preachers, lawyers, and doctors. Anyone owning property bordering it.

They would trot out the usual gods: Tax Base, Retail Sales, Jobs. Never mind that a "partnership" of this sort customarily bestows huge tax breaks

on the developer, the retail dollars depart for other places, and the good
jobs—construction—are temporary, while low-paying jobs like those of
the girls at the perfume counters will stay.

As I walked back it began to rain. The kind of morning that would bring
Richard Simmons down. Back at the office, I poured another cup of coffee,
sat, and shook my head. If the project didn't die, we were in for a long ride,
and opponents would need a decent attorney.

I lunched at the Mediterranean, and found among other attorneys only
mild curiosity—certainly no outrage like mine. Even a bowl of Papa's
vegetable soup didn't warm my heart.

But it didn't take long for opposition to boil up. Some folks—a few
business owners, an artist or two, several tenants, with more youth than
age, more worry than optimism—soon formed Save Downtown Asheville
(SDA). This was in the old days, when a few doctors still made house calls
and reporters actually attended meetings, so an article next morning said
SDA planned to fight this proposal tooth and toenail. I hoped they would
find my office.

They did. Over the next year and a half those rascals did something
that to my knowledge had never happened in our town. They fought City
Hall—and won.

I take little credit for that. My pro bono time was much more entertaining than corporate law. SDA didn't have much fun at first. They did
not begin from strength. Their officers were a furniture delivery man with
thinning hair, a couple of tenants of the aforesaid Canadian, one who sold
pricey paper things and the other macramé (I said the city had encouraged
very small businesses), and a sharp young property owner who reminded
me of Joan Baez. They struck me as about as political as a yard full of
roosters, but they had energy, determination, and grit. And three of them
were local.

For nearly two years, SDA attended every meeting of city council, the
housing authority, planning and zoning, and the AREDC. They made notes,

spoke at public hearings and civic clubs, asked council for money (which, of course, they did not get), talked, organized, wrote letters to national publications, asked "Sixty Minutes" to run a story, made friends with HUD staff in Greensboro and Washington. I was impressed.

Soon after SDA was formed, something called the Committee of 36 announced support for the mall. Chaired by an ex-mayor, they were the usual suspects—bankers, merchants, and wealthy folks normally in the woodwork but trotted out for really big deals, like Confederate veterans in another era.

On the other side? Artists, hippies, renters, students, little old ladies in tennis shoes, preservationists, soreheads, misanthropes, moviegoers, anyone who had ever been screwed by local government. They began to call themselves the Committee of a Thousand.

To dramatize the size of the project, an artist, after Christo, organized an April "Wrap" of downtown, at which hundreds of volunteers held up yellow fabric around the mall boundary. This made the television news.

SDA focused on how much this train wreck would cost: $40 million of taxpayer money, to acquire property and prepare the site. The city entertained various other funding options, their favorite being revenue bonds, which do not require a referendum.

One can't have a federal redevelopment area without a certain percentage of "blighted" properties, so the city's building inspectors began to nose around the area. (Duplicate inspections were done by a private firm, also paid by the city.) In spite of the fact that everyone had Certificates of Occupancy, and the chief inspector thought the project a waste of time and money, we had a good idea what his report would say.

We knew a lot of things, because a mole in the planning department fed us invaluable information. (Early on, when an official insisted there was no firm timetable for the mall, an interior designer unfurled a leaked flow chart and demanded clarification. Such an embarrassed city official has seldom been seen.) Our mole was soon suspected and fed misinformation.

(Two or three other malls planned for the area! A Disney theme park is coming! The sky is falling!) At times this whole fracas resembled a spy story starring the Keystone Kops.

All began to come to a head during the summer of 1980. The developer unveiled a model of the thing in July. It reminded me of Moby Dick. No, that's not exactly right. The whale was an extrovert. This thing looked inward. A suburban-style mall, with high, forbidding walls, sitting atop a subterranean parking garage, with—cue the rattlesnakes—an office tower midship. With a straight face, the developer said, "This is not a mall. It is basically a restoration and renovation of the downtown." Yeah, and I was Little Bo Peep.

In August the city declared the project feasible "at this point in time." The buildings were officially blighted in November, despite conflicting reports. The housing authority was designated the redevelopment agency, the city had applied for an Urban Development Action Grant, and everything pointed toward a gaping hole soon appearing downtown.

Then the state's Local Government Commission ruled the city could not use revenue bonds.

The afternoon SDA came with the news, their chairman looked like he'd been rode hard and put up wet. All of them had been working too hard and worrying too much. But you do that when livelihood's at stake. "They're going to use general obligations," he said. "What now?"

He looked so apprehensive I couldn't help but laugh. "How loud can you holler 'Pleeeeeze don't throw me in the briar patch?' GOBs require a referendum. Do you think for a minute John Q. Citizen will approve that kind of crap? Let's celebrate." We toasted our good fortune with some beer and red wine.

Developer and city council had been close to making as ruinous a contract as ever bound pimp and whore. I had figured ways to delay if they'd used revenue bonds, but I feared we'd ultimately lose that fight. What a great gift. Almost restored my faith in government. Almost.

We set up a second organization, Taxpayers Against Bonds, to run the political campaign in late September 1981. That board of directors included prominent West Ashevillians (who generally felt the city treated them like red-headed stepchildren), various salt-of-the-earth types, some even from North Asheville. Our foot soldiers stuffed envelopes, raised money, made window signs for condemned buildings, placed ads in the paper, wrote newsletters. Pure grassroots energy.

Then someone (I'd love to think it was the pro-mall folks) had a brilliant idea—a broadcast town meeting on the referendum question. October 22 at First Baptist Church. We used our three weeks wisely. TV people—not from WLOS, whose bosses supported the mall—coached us on makeup, how to act relaxed but authoritative, what questions to avoid without seeming to, which to jump on like a chicken on a June bug. We even practiced answering the questions with which we planned to salt the audience.

Their side—now calling themselves Building a Better Asheville, and pushing the "Asheville Commercial Center"—didn't rehearse at all. It showed. For an hour and a half they dodged questions, looking sweaty, suspicious. We had fun for an hour and a half.

On November 3, 1981, the voters spoke. A fine day in the history of Asheville. That night Gatsby's bar and grill began to fill with nervous people, pacing about, standing at the bar, eating supper, smoking, making small talk. The returns began to come in (this was before the Internet) about ten, and by eleven we began to relax and celebrate a hard-fought victory. The bonds failed by two to one.

There was a time when this project would or would not have flown on the word of the city manager. It would simply have been announced. I really think that the folks in City Hall thought they could ramrod one more project. Thank God they were wrong.

Interesting how memory works. "I knew it wouldn't fly," said one vocal mall supporter years later. "It was a bad idea from the start," said another.

My greatest satisfaction from the fight happened ten or twelve years later, when the chair of the "36" hailed me on the street, draped his madras-covered arm around my shoulder, and said, "You know, I was wrong. I admit it. Just look around."

It gets my goat that in the last twenty years, several histories of Asheville have been published, none of which mentions Save Downtown Asheville. The cliché is that winners write history, but this is different. Somehow Asheville has chosen simply to forget those two years of acrimony. They act as though the mayor's commission that got a new ball rolling was hatched from nothing, like the good Lord spoke creation into being.

SDA people gave two years of their lives to defeating a dragon. Some who do that, like St. George, are canonized. SDA seems to have been forgotten. They deserve better. A historical marker. A key to the city. At least a bloody footnote.

The other night Rosa Jane and I ventured downtown for dinner. The streets were full. People goofing around, busking, strolling in the lights, shopping, having a good time. Reminded me of New Orleans without the bars that brag that their girls are guys. A weekday evening, too. (I no longer go downtown on weekends. I'm old enough to worry about breaking something if I misstep trying to avoid an enthusiastic reveler.)

Blight? Bah, humbug. Asheville is now a vibrant, busy place. I'm glad I played a small part in making sure a town remained for sensible developers to renovate. But I am wary. The population is growing again, in percentages not seen since the decades after the trains first came. I love and enjoy Asheville, but still watch for rattlesnakes.

---

**WAYNE CALDWELL** was born and raised in Asheville and, except for some years in the academy, has lived there all his life. He is the author of two novels, *Cataloochee* and *Requiem by Fire* (winner of the 2010 Thomas Wolfe Memorial Literary Award from the WNC Historical Association), several short stories, and a poem or two. In 1980–1981, he was chair of Save Downtown Asheville.

# Baghdad on the French Broad: Zebulon Baird Vance's Asheville

SHARYN McCRUMB

*Asheville?* Why, in my salad days that bustling little mountain town was as marvelous to me as a Baghdad on the French Broad. Although I was born only a few miles away, I was nearing twenty years of age before I went to live there. With a place as grand as Asheville, you have to work up to it, gradual. Looking back on it now, I suppose it was only an upstart frontier town with glorified notions of itself, but my residence there, and the connections I made during that time, paved my way to the Governor's Palace in Raleigh and on to the marble halls of Congress in Washington.

After the war, and an uneasy few months in the old Capitol Prison, I got elected governor again, and then I went back to Congress. I roosted in the U.S. Senate forever after, which required that I spend most of my time in Washington, so I never lived in Asheville again, but I went back when I could, and in the prosperity of my later years, I built a fine summer residence, Gombroom, in proximity of it.

I was a country boy, born in 1831 during the term of Andrew Jackson, our first backcountry president, and bred in the little settlement on Reems Creek, back in the wilds of Buncombe County, a place so small that it was only on the map two days a week. I reveled in the freedom of that mountain fastness, and whatever time I could steal from farm chores and lessons at Uncle Nehemiah Blackstock's little school, I spent fishing, and hunting, and rambling in those endless woods. In those days the pockets of my little patched trousers bulged with fish-worms and matches, marbles and kite-strings, and I wished for no life more regimented than this.

The rustic idyll of my boyhood was interrupted by a sojourn at Washington College just over the mountain into Tennessee, and that spate of formal education ended once and for all with the death of my father, when I was a lad of eleven. After that Mother gathered up her brood of young Vances, and took us over the ridge to a community called Lapland *(by 1851, it was called Marshall, the county seat of newly minted Madison County),* where she endeavored to support the family by running a hostelry for the drovers who ran stock, mostly hogs, from the western ranges through our mountain passes to sell in the big eastern cities. I got one sort of rough and ready education from those drovers, and I think it helped me in later life, when politicking obliged me to speak to all manner of folk to get myself elected. My "finishing school," though, and the royal road to my advancement in polite society took place at a nearby resort: the Warm Springs Hotel, where the gentry came to escape from the fevers and miasmas of the flatland summer.

I got myself hired on there as a gangly adolescent, clerking for Mr. John E. Patton, who owned the resort. The hotel was a white wood-frame structure, two stories high, with columns and long, covered porches, standing in a long meadow where the waters of a wide creek flowed into the French Broad River. Mr. Patton might have wondered why a rawboned boy of sixteen would seek work at a hotel, when there were drovers jobs aplenty for a hardy youth—certainly a more appealing way to support

140

a widowed mother and the younger ones at home. The stockman's life held many charms for a country youth: horses to ride, the freedom of the wilderness, and the untrammeled adventures with the drovers on the trail. But from my mother's side of the family I inherited the Scots' practicality, coupled with the fever of ambition that runs through the Vance bloodline, so, despite the lure of the drovers' road, I chose the path of self-improvement.

Those months of clerking at the hotel served me well in later life. The place was my own private zoo, full of rich people from the eastern seaboard, and I studied them the way Mr. Audubon studied birds, until I learned the language of gentility. I mended my speech, so that I could say "hors d'oeuvres" instead of "horse-overs," "perspire" instead of "sweat," and "passed away" instead of "died." It was just like learning a foreign language, but those phrases were the passwords into the aristocracy, so by god I learned them.

Presently, when I reached the age of eighteen, my mother sold the hostelry, and moved the family to Asheville, for she despaired of raising a crop of ladies and gentlemen in the society of rustics and drovers. By then I thought I had been sanded down enough by Warm Springs gentility to venture into polite society, so after a few years of wild oats and idleness, I determined to seek out an attorney in Asheville and embark upon the study of law under his tutelage. Now, as a rough-hewn mountain boy, I might have been more timorous about taking up residence in the great frontier town of Asheville, except for one thing: My ancestors had practically built the place.

My father's father was David Vance, and in the Carolina backcountry, that was a name to conjure with. He had fought alongside General Washington in the Revolution, at Brandywine, Germantown, and Monmouth, and he braved the winter at Valley Forge. Then late in the war, when he was sent back to North Carolina, he had joined the Overmountain Men, and fought at Kings Mountain, down on the South Carolina border, where the Loyalist forces were defeated in an hour—the first colonial victory in a long campaign that the Continental army up north had mostly been losing. That was in 1780.

When the war finally ended, Grandfather Vance was elected to the North Carolina General Assembly, and, when he wore himself out in politics, he retired to a thousand-acre farm in Buncombe County, where I was born nigh onto fifty years after Kings Mountain. When my grandfather died, he left us a library of nearly five hundred books—everything from sermons to Shakespeare to Roman history. Those were the books that my mother read to us children when I was growing up. Grandfather's other great legacy was some of the land on which the city of Asheville was built. Another chunk of it was built upon land purchased from my mother's family, the Bairds, so in Asheville, if nowhere else on earth, I could count myself a prince.

I might have mentioned Colonel David Vance a time or two when I was seeking a position of study with a local attorney. I had less to say about some of my other relatives: Great-Aunt Rebecca who had been scalped in an Indian attack, but survived it, none the worse for wear, except for a little bald patch on the crown of her head; and my father's eldest brother, Robert, who became so enraged at losing an election to the U.S. Congress that he challenged the winner, Sam Carson, to a duel. Sam Carson won that round as well, and Uncle Robert Vance died of his wounds. Since his opponent was coached in marksmanship by his fellow Congressman Davy Crockett, the outcome of the duel is scarcely to be wondered at. I almost tried it myself in the heat of Buncombe County politicking, but cooler heads prevailed. Just as well. When the war came, I learned that I liked talking a good deal better than fighting.

We were a storied family, and when people inquired about my bloodlines, I could hold forth for longer than they cared to listen. Thus fortified with that pedigree and a fair amount of book-learning, I set out to make something of myself and to leave my mark upon Asheville.

At the time I took up residency in the town, Asheville was a bustling little community of more than four hundred souls, plus a goodly number of summer visitors, who came, just as they had frequented Warm Springs, for the cool air of a mountain summer. The Buncombe Turnpike, the stage-coach road that led on to the resort at Warm Springs and onward over the mountains to Greeneville, Tennessee, passed through the town, depositing visitors in the fine hotels on Eagle Street and North Main. Since Asheville was the county seat of Buncombe, the circuit court met there, and the political powers of western North Carolina were concentrated within its borders. The people who were elected and sent out to serve in the govern-ments of the state capital and of Washington were chosen here, and by and large they resided here. For a likely young man with ambition, the place was an orchard of opportunity, and if I did not avail myself of that bounty, I would have been a fool as well as a sluggard.

When I was younger, it was easy enough to glory in the idleness of sleepy little Lapland, for I felt neither envy nor inferiority to the farmers and drovers that constituted society in those parts—I quite liked them— but Asheville was a different story. The summer guests at the Warm Springs Hotel had been easy to charm for a day or a week, and they were civil enough, but perhaps it was because I was not part of their real social milieu. They always went away, back to Charleston, or Richmond, or Wilmington, leaving me little but a few more lessons in how to comport myself among the gentry. Asheville society stayed put, and that was another matter altogether.

The city contained a veritable ladder of aristocracy, and it was soon clear to me that I was not very many rungs from the bottom. At eighteen I had no money and I had trained for no profession—thus I had no prospects. As I walked along the streets of Asheville, I saw the fine carriages of the local gentry and visitors from the eastern seaboard. I gazed at the stately pillared homes fronting the tree-lined boulevards, and I thought of our family's humble little frame house on a far less fashionable street. I knew myself to be a plebian, cast adrift among the patricians.

Every week the Buck and the Eagle, those two elegant hotels that hosted the Buncombe Turnpike's stagecoach travelers, would hold elegant dances for the local young people of good family. It did not matter that I could dance as well as any fellow in the county, or that I counted myself a tall and handsome young man. The hotel soirées were events from which I— a nobody—would be barred.

It didn't take me long to learn that I could not abide the feeling of being outranked and excluded. The very idea of being disdained by people no smarter or better bred than I was unendurable, but I thought I had sufficient wit and determination to alter my situation, and in Asheville my pedigree should be sufficient.

144

So at the age of twenty, I resolved to abandon my boisterous ways and to devote myself to the study of law, so that I could contribute more to politics than a drunken advocacy at a country polling site.

Thus, one December afternoon in 1850 I found myself hat in hand in the parlor of Mr. John E. Woodfin, one of Buncombe County's most able attorneys, asking to be taken on as a student. So it was that I began my personal journey on the high road to fame and fortune, and I never looked back. Like the Buncombe Turnpike, my road to prosperity led through Asheville, past the steep and perilous mountains, and left me far indeed from the sheltering hills of North Carolina. I never forgot them, though. They were my first love.

**SHARYN McCRUMB** is an award-winning writer, best known for her Appalachian "Ballad" novels, including the *New York Times* bestsellers *The Ballad of Frankie Silver, She Walks These Hills,* and *The Ballad of Tom Dooley,* and for *St. Dale,* winner of a Library of Virginia Award and named "Best Appalachian Novel" in 2005. In 2008, Sharyn McCrumb was named a Virginia Woman of History for Achievement in Literature. This story is based on material from her novel *Ghost Riders,* winner of the national Audie Award for Best Recorded Novel and the Wilma Dykeman Award for Historical Fiction. (The paperback edition of *Ghost Riders* was published by John F. Blair, Publisher.)

# Vote

An excerpt from *Backside of the Country*

SARAH WILLIAMS

IN NOVEMBER 1945, Annie Jo packed the family's meager belongings and moved to Asheville. She thought they were moving up North. She soon learned that not only were they still in the South, but also that many of the racial barriers she thought they'd left in Mississippi existed in North Carolina. Eartha and Ronald promised to write to her often and to visit as soon as they could make enough money to purchase tickets.

As she rode with the children in tow, Daisy became fretful. Annie Jo finally realized that she couldn't breastfeed. Her milk had dried. She knew little to nothing about the human anatomy, so when the bus stopped at a small store, she went in and bought a quart of milk. She drank most of it, thinking that it would travel down her throat and into her breasts, and then she'd be able to feed Daisy. Junior drank some of it, but Annie Jo drank the largest portion. Daisy continued to fret, which Annie Jo didn't understand because usually she was a good baby.

When they stepped off the bus in Asheville, Annie Jo was relieved to see Wilbur. She blurted, "I hope you know a doctor because there's something wrong with Daisy! She whined almost the entire trip! She's sick, Wilbur!"

She looked ill herself. He noticed her distress and hugged her. "I'll ask Mrs. Young when we get home," he said. "More than likely she knows a doctor who'll see Daisy."

Annie Jo was fascinated by the view as they rode toward her new home. She became reverently silent as they traveled. The city wasn't at its peak of beauty at that time of year, but to the virgin eye, it was quite beautiful. Though they rode on relatively flat land, she noticed that they were surrounded by statuesque mountains and old buildings that boasted the wonders of bygone architecture. She had never seen anything like it, for she'd always lived on flat land and had never been far from home. As Wilbur drove through downtown, Annie Jo stared at quaint little shops that displayed stylish mannequin-clad figures that were different from anything she'd ever known. She was completely quiet and was pleased to have moved to such a town.

They arrived home and walked into a house that by many people's standards was well kept but average. But to Annie Jo, it was breathtaking. She'd never known colored people who lived in such luxury. Wilbur told Mrs. Young about Daisy's condition when they first walked in.

She asked, "Could she be hungry?"

Annie Jo didn't think so, and she explained what she'd done on the bus to try to make Daisy comfortable. Mrs. Young laughed loudly, but Annie Jo found no humor in the situation, for she was worried about her baby. At any other time, she would have given Mrs. Young, a small, petite, fifty-six-year-old woman who possessed a very attractive figure and face, a compliment. But Mrs. Young could see from Annie Jo's expression that she didn't find anything entertaining about the matter. She had to clarify why she'd laughed. "I'm not laughing at you, young lady, I'm laughing at how frustrated you've become. When you drink milk, it doesn't go to your breasts, so I'm sure Daisy is hungry, because she hasn't eaten anything since you left Mississippi. Do you have a bottle?"

In her Mississippi brogue, Annie Jo responded, "No, I've been breast-feeding her, so I haven't had a reason to buy bottles."

Mrs. Young had noticed Annie Jo's faulty grammar and decided it was her duty to help her to improve. Mrs. Young, who tended children to supplement her income, was sure she had a bottle around somewhere. She found one, boiled it, filled it, and fed Daisy. The baby began to behave the way she usually did; she was happy and jolly. Annie Jo had learned something that day about her body. Later, Mrs. Young helped her to prepare the children for bed. Although she believed that Mrs. Young had laughed at her, Annie Jo felt herself becoming fond of her.

Wilbur worked hard six days a week but drew a good salary and was a good provider. Annie Jo had talked to Mrs. Young about keeping the children if she could find a job and Mrs. Young agreed. She knew that Annie Jo was a young, energetic woman and needed to get out of the house sometimes. Annie Jo asked Wilbur if it would be okay if she found a job. The thought of her working didn't thrill him, but he also knew that he couldn't keep her confined to the house. She believed that if they both worked they'd be able to rent their own house. It didn't take her long to find a job. She was hired to run an elevator in a department store.

It was during that time that she questioned the necessity of her and her brothers taking all the shots they'd taken when they were younger. She was required to take a physical in order to be hired at the store. Taking the physical produced fear in her because the thought took her back to that horrendous time in her life [when she and other African Americans in rural Mississippi took part in a government-sponsored experimental syphilis treatment program]. How could she be positive that the disease had been cured? If it showed up in her blood, she wouldn't get the job. She needed to work, so it was a chance she had to take. She'd been told that she'd been cured, but was she really?

Great relief washed over her when she was hired. She'd never truly know whether she'd really had the disease. Would they have made them take shots for all those months for nothing? They had nothing to gain by it. She must've had the disease because white people wouldn't have given them the shots free unless they were afraid of the disease spreading. They were told that one way of contracting the disease was through sexual contact. Many white married men had sex with colored women, so that could have been a reason for giving the shots free.

Other colored women worked at the department store where she was hired and they all became friends. They began to socialize on a regular basis.

148

Annie Jo and Wilbur wanted to rent a house and they began to house-hunt. Houses used as rental property in colored communities were few and far between. Finally, in 1946, they found a two-family house. An elderly lady, Mrs. Cameron, lived on the lower level. She didn't seem to like children when they first moved there, but later, Annie Jo realized that she really liked their kids. She simply got a kick out of complaining.

Moving into their own place allowed them to invite people over for card parties, and it gave Wilbur freedom to drink with their friends, who always joked about Wilbur being the first to get drunk. They liked him when he was high, because he'd tell them strange but funny stories about their life in Mississippi.

They had never heard of can heat, but they listened intently as he talked about helping his uncle make it. Can heat was a quick and cheap high. Their friends believed that he could save them money if he made some for them. Wilbur never told them the ingredients needed to make this drink, because he had no desire to drink it again.

From force of habit, Annie Jo listened to the news every night. It seemed strange to hear Asheville mentioned so often. Colored people and whites were separated from one another in Asheville too, but the fear of whites that had pervaded their everyday existence in Mississippi seemed to be absent in colored people in North Carolina.

She'd heard the people they knew make negative comments about whites, but they didn't dwell on it.

When they left Mississippi, the economy was terrible, but listening to the radio taught her that every state in the nation wasn't opposed to change. North Carolina had taken advantage of Roosevelt's New Deal and the advantages to be gained during the war years. The governor of North Carolina when she moved there was R. Gregg Cherry. [According to one radio commentator:] "The people who held conservative views before the war had a mindset change. They were ready to move forward at a steady pace. Governor Cherry held on to conservative views which did not please the discontented public. He had raised the budget of state agencies, expanded the medical school at the University of North Carolina, and added more beds to the state's many hospitals, but these were considered to be moderate changes. The people wanted better roads, improved schools, and colored people wanted equal treatment and better job opportunities. These requests seemed to be beyond Cherry's abilities and vision."

Things seemed to Annie Jo, and according to the news, very progressive for residents of North Carolina, but she didn't have a complete understanding of the status of colored people in her new home. One day when she went to visit Mrs. Young, she decided to talk about it. Mrs. Young was a retired schoolteacher whom Annie Jo felt would be able to explain many things, and she was.

Mrs. Young loved falling back into her role as a teacher. She explained, "Things aren't great for colored people here. I'm aware that in Mississippi whites have a bad habit of hanging us. We don't worry about that here, but colored men have to keep their distance from white women. Most of us can sense, by the way white women look at colored men, they they'd like to experiment with them, but those who take a chance, if caught, will scream rape. Then colored men are sent to prison for a long time. Colored men have a good reason to be afraid of the white female.

"Most colored people can't get jobs that pay decent wages. Wilbur, working for the V.A. Hospital, has one of the better jobs, and so do people who work for the railroad. Most colored people work in white homes. It's honest work so I guess they shouldn't complain. There are a few doctors, lawyers, and teachers who live here who were fortunate to be able to attend college. They're able to make a pretty good living."

Annie Jo said, "I've heard the word *college* mentioned a couple of times, but I'm not sure what they are. I believe they're good, but what are they, and where are the plantations around here?"

"Colleges are schools that people attend after they graduate high school. They go in order to learn how to do something other than working in white homes. The people who are able to graduate are usually paid more money than those who work in white homes."

"Can I go to one of those colleges?" Annie Jo asked.

"Anybody who's finished high school can go, but you have to pay to go."

"I guess I can't go then, because I didn't finish high school. We didn't go as long each year as white children did anyway, because we had to work on plantations to help make money to live."

"That's the problem for most colored children. They must work to help their families survive. You might not be able to go to college, but you can learn to speak better. When you're here, listen to the way I pronounce words, and listen to the way people on the radio pronounce their words, then your grammar will improve."

"You talk like white peoples here in Asheville talk. White peoples in Mississippi talk like uses."

"You mean people and us."

"I mean peoples and uses. Um talkin' 'bout moe dan one. I learnt dat much in school."

"The words *people* and *us* refer to more than one person, so you don't have to say *peoples* and *uses* to mean more than one. Also the words *dan* and *dat* begin with *th* rather than *d*. The words are *than* and *that*."

"Um gone try to 'memba dat, I mean that."

"We'll work on it slowly. You have time."

"Okay, um gone 'memba people, us, than, and that. If I say dem . . . them wrong when um here, tell me, okay?"

"It's a deal. You asked me where the plantations are around here. We don't have many farms here. The larger ones are located in the eastern part of the state."

Using her Mississippi way of talking, she said, "I like you, Mrs. Young, and I'm glad that I've met you. I know you're going to help me to talk like you. Thank you."

Junior ran into the room and hugged his mother. He was so cute and animated as he blurted, "We had fun today, Mama, but Daisy hit her big toe! Mrs. Young told her to keep her shoes on, but she didn't! She crawled near that table and threw her legs out! Her big toe hit the table and she screamed so loud!"

Annie Jo looked at Daisy's normal-looking toe and rubbed it. She would've kissed it to make it better, but it was too dirty. About five minutes later she gathered them up and she and Junior walked home. She carried Daisy. They lived only a couple of blocks from Mrs. Young's house. Her beautiful children brought her so much joy and they were very active. As they walked, Junior continued to tell her about their day, and she smiled as she listened to his charming little voice.

---

In June, Annie Jo gave birth to Ernest. Wilbur came to the hospital to visit her that day. He'd gone to the nursery to see the baby before going to Annie Jo's room. When she saw him, he looked elated. He kissed her then said gratefully, "Thank you for giving me another son. When are they planning to let you out? I'll get Boyce or Adam to bring me to get you. Mrs. Young kept the kids last night, and they were excited about staying with her. She was more than willing to keep them."

As he talked, she could smell stale alcohol on his breath, and she knew why Mrs. Young had been more than willing to keep them. She asked, "Have you spent any time with them since I've been here? It was the perfect time to get close to them again."

"No I haven't spent any time with them. We've been so excited about our new baby that we've been celebrating."

"I want you to go by Mrs. Young's house, get the children, and take them to the park. They need time with you. You'll be making friends for the rest of your life, but you can't replace your children. They need you now, while they're young, to be a good father. Go get them and show them that you love them."

"Okay, I will, but they'll be with her again tonight because I have things to do." He understood exactly what she was saying, but to do what she meant for him to do would make him unhappy. He had interests outside of his home that he wasn't willing to give up.

Later that day Larry came by the hospital. Annie Jo was pleased to see him, but his visit also made her uneasy. She touched his hand and asked him to sit down. She had to explain her skepticism about him visiting her. "I'm glad to see you, but what if Wilbur comes back? If he sees you, he's going to be furious. He's jealous of you and I don't think he'll be able to handle seeing you here."

"Wilbur won't be back today. I know this because I saw him with Boyce and Sandy. He's already high. Anyway, I've missed you and would've taken that chance. He wouldn't worry about me if he paid more attention to home. I'm glad that I have the potential to be his worst nightmare. He needs to appreciate what he's got. When will you leave here?"

He felt that he and Annie Jo could have a good life together, but he couldn't tell her that because he didn't want to frighten her. He wanted her but the likelihood of hurting others couldn't be ignored. He wouldn't tell her how much he loved her unless an opportunity presented itself.

She responded, "The doctor said that since I'm healing properly I'll be able to go home tomorrow. I believe I'll be able to take the kids to the park Saturday of next week. I hate that I have to sneak to see you."

Larry knew that Wilbur wanted it all and had it all. Wilbur was seeing Sandy regularly, but he wasn't about to let Annie Jo have that same freedom.

He looked at her angelic but disturbed face, and he wanted to take her in his arms to protect her from all harm. Unfortunately, that wasn't possible. He told her to be patient, that one day things would work out to their advantage.

She said, "I hope so. You do know that if we keep this up we're going to get caught, don't you. That's simply the way things work out."

Although Annie Jo couldn't take the children to the park Saturday of the week she returned home, she was able to visit Mrs. Young. When she arrived, Mrs. Young was sitting comfortably in her living room listening to the news. She asked where the baby was. Mrs. Cameron was babysitting him, Annie Jo told her, because she was in no condition to carry him. Mrs. Young asked Annie Jo to relax and listen to the news with her. They listened while the children went to the children's room to play.

On the radio, the reporter said, "North Carolina is a Democratic state which has a Democratic government that is moderate in its approach. During the Great Depression, President Roosevelt led the nation on a liberal course. As the election of 1948 approaches, people of the state wonder if North Carolina will continue on its moderate path or move toward more liberal policies. A North Carolina liberal, W. Kerr Scott, is challenging a moderate Democrat, Charles M. Johnson. Scott claims to be the choice of the common people and refers to these people as 'the Branch-Head Boys.' They live away from the seat of government. Farmers prefer Scott because he wants to bring electricity to rural areas. Industrial workers prefer him because he believes that unions should have the right to bargain with management for better pay and working conditions for employees.

"Negroes support him even though he hasn't said anything about ridding the state of the old Jim Crow laws that discriminate against them, but he hasn't tried to get support from whites by attacking Negroes, as many politicians have done. He plans for many of his public works programs to benefit Negroes as well as whites."

Mrs. Young said, "I know that this Scott fellow is white, but it's about time that a politician put Negroes in his plans. I'm going to vote for him based on what little he says he'll do for us. He might not ever do those things, but at least he's thought enough of us to mention us, in a positive manner, in his campaign speeches. Who do you plan to vote for, Annie Jo?"

"I've never voted, Mrs. Young. What will I have to do to be able to vote?"

"I'll go with you to register. You must register in order to vote and you must pay a poll tax. I'll pay that for you. What are you doing tomorrow? They'll be registering people at the playground tomorrow between nine o'clock and one. How well do you read?"

"I can read, why?"

"I'm going to give you a paper. It contains the Preamble to the Constitution." Annie Jo shrugged her shoulders thinking that she didn't know what a Preamble to the Constitution was, but she'd read it.

Mrs. Young went into another room and returned carrying a sheet of paper. She gave it to Annie Jo and said, "Read it to me."

Annie Jo began, "We the people of the United States . . ." She stumbled on the words *tranquility* and *posterity*, but Mrs. Young helped her. She was embarrassed because she'd stumbled, but she'd practice then read it flawlessly the next day. "You'll be proud of me, Mrs. Young."

Mrs. Young was already proud of her. She said, "It's not important that I be proud of you, but it is most important that you'll be proud of yourself. Read it, practice, and we'll get you registered tomorrow."

Annie Jo asked, "What happened between you and Wilbur? He didn't sound too happy when I told him that I was planning to visit you."

"He didn't tell you?"

"No, I asked but he wouldn't say."

"Then maybe I shouldn't say anything. He's already upset with me, and I don't want to make him angrier then he already is. He said some things to me that weren't very nice, but I suppose I wasn't very nice either."

"If he's not telling me and neither are you, how will I ever know?"

"I'll tell you but you must promise not to throw it in his face." Annie Jo promised, although, depending on what Mrs. Young had to say, she didn't know if she could keep the promise.

"He came by here one night and he'd been drinking. I asked if he really wanted to see his kids in his condition. He told me that they were his damn kids, and if I didn't watch myself, he'd take them with him. I certainly didn't want him to do that, so I went and got them. He hugged them and Junior said, 'You smell funny, Daddy. What have you been eating?' Wilbur thought that what Junior had said was funny, so he laughed then tripped and fell. Daisy thought he was playing, so she stepped on his stomach. He shouted, 'Get off of me, girl! I'm your daddy and I'm not going to let you disrespect me like that! Then he hit her and she cried.

"I yelled, 'Get out of here Wilbur, and don't come back until you're sober and clean.'

"He snapped, 'Come on, Sandy. We don't have to stay here to hear this old bitch.' She laughed as if he'd said the cleverest thing, then they left. It took me quite awhile to get Daisy calmed."

Annie Jo apologized, then she told her how Wilbur was constantly angry. She also told her that she wouldn't talk to him about it, because she didn't want Mrs. Young to be afraid that he'd later approach her about it.

Annie Jo collected the children and they prepared to leave. Mrs. Young asked, "How can you stand living with him if he's drinking like that regularly?"

Annie Jo explained that she was trying to hang on because he was the children's father, plus she needed his help with child support. He was a good provider, but that wasn't a good excuse for him to hit while he was angry.

Mrs. Young offered her house to them rent-free, for their children were like her grandchildren. Annie Jo couldn't promise that she'd move in, but she was grateful that Mrs. Young had offered her an outlet.

As they walked home, she thought about Wilbur and Sandy who'd been introduced as Boyce's girlfriend. She'd had her doubts which triggered the thought that some nights he could've come home smelling of Sandy's perfume.

After dinner, she went into their bedroom and studied the paper Mrs. Young had given her. Wilbur walked in and asked what she was doing. She said, "Listen to me read this because I have to read it perfectly by tomorrow."

"Why do you have to read it?"

"I'm going to register to vote tomorrow, and I have to read this in order to register."

"Why are you going to register to vote tomorrow? Your choices are all white men. Think about it. Name at least one white politician who has, even in some small way, done anything for us."

"I can't, but I want to vote, Wilbur, so don't try to make me believe that voting is stupid."

"It is stupid, and I'll never understand why Negroes bother. Things don't change just because we decide to vote. White people don't want us to vote anyway. Look at you, taking time to learn to read that old stupid paper. You've been listening to that radio too much. I should make you stop, because it's making you think like white people, and that's dangerous, girl."

"How can I think like white people when I've never been white?" she protested. "I don't think they'll do all kinds of things for us, but one might come along who will, and I want to do my part to get him elected. I like having the freedom to vote if I want to. If I don't vote, then I don't have the right to complain about the politicians who are elected."

"I'm going to complain even if I don't vote," Wilbur said, "because I have the freedom to do that. I know I'm not going to waste my time standing in a line waiting to vote, and I'm not going to subject myself to white insults. It's not worth it."

They went to the playground the next day. Mrs. Young paid the poll tax then watched the children while Annie Jo went inside to register. When she finished she went outside to sit with Mrs. Young as the children played.

"How do you feel as a registered voter?" Mrs. Young asked.

"I feel great, but I'll feel even better in November when I'll actually vote. I have a question, though. There was a young white lady standing in the white line who registered too. She didn't have to read the Preamble. Why?"

"I never said anything is fair and equal. Expect things like that. It would be good if we could talk Wilbur into registering."

"Forget it, Mrs. Young, because he's not at all interested."

Mrs. Young listened to her and was proud of the way she'd conquered her grammar deficiency. She commented on it and Annie Jo thanked her, because Mrs. Young had moved her to the place where she realized that she really did need to improve her use of the language.

"We need to talk other Negroes into registering," Mrs. Young said.

**SARAH WILLIAMS** is the author of the novel *Backside of the Country,* from which this View is excerpted. A former language arts teacher, she grew up in Asheville. She began writing after she recovered from an aneurysm in 1992.

# House of Twigs

HEATHER NEWTON

SHERMAN HALL sucks on a Certs, waiting for his wife Josie to register the last person who has come to this free seminar on How to Build Your Own Log Home. Out of fifty who signed up at the Asheville Home Show only a dozen have shown up. Sherman prefers to talk to yuppies, who are as ignorant as he is about construction techniques and joinery. Instead tonight he faces mountain men, their hands hardened by years of under-the-table carpentry work. Such men always ask questions Sherman doesn't know the answers to. He checks to make sure Clive is stationed and ready beside a stack of sample cedar, pine, and cypress. Clive is cut from the same timber as the guys in the audience. Sherman pays Clive to grunt technical answers when Sherman flashes him a particular "help-me-out-of-this-one" hand signal.

Sherman is tall and good-looking. He wears a full beard like his hero and fellow Illinoisan, Abraham Lincoln, though Lincoln was thin and Sherman is not. Tonight Sherman wears Italian-cut pants and a gold bracelet that speaks of the wealth to be made from owning a log home franchise. He checks the audience for attractive women, a habit he's fallen into since he turned forty last year. Most of the women in the Days Inn conference room are overweight and uniformly permed. They are here because their steady salaries give them power over family purse strings. There is one pretty face, a young woman with light blue eyes and honey-streaked hair that touches her waist. She sits expectantly beside a skinny husband who is no more than a kid. Sherman knows from experience that for this couple a log home is an alternative to a trailer in some parent's front yard. He gives the girl his warmest smile and gets one in return. He sucks in his stomach as Josie closes the door and motions for him to begin.

Log homes sell to married couples, and he and Josie have perfected a spiel that shows what a strong married couple they are. He starts with a practiced intro about the cost of log homes as compared to conventional frame houses, the resistance of cedar to insects, the merits of cypress over bowing pine. Josie works the PowerPoint presentation. The audience stares hungrily at gleaming redwood and cathedral windows that cost more than any one of them makes in a month.

"Honey," Sherman calls to Josie, "tell them about the hot tub we've installed in our own 2,000-square-foot Lincoln Log Home."

"Sure, Sweetie." Josie follows their script. "It has a remote control that we carry with us in our car. When we're twenty minutes from home, we activate the control and the water is hot by the time we roll into our driveway."

The audience murmurs appreciatively. A tiny smile plays around the mouth of the pretty, blue-eyed girl as she thinks about soaking in that hot tub. Sherman catches her eye and almost winks. "Of course, you'll prob-ably want to start out a little more basic than that. That's the beauty of a Lincoln Log Home. You can order it as simple or as fancy as you like, and we can build as much of it for you as you like. Some people want to do everything but the electrical and plumbing themselves. Others are happy to have us put up the whole thing. We can develop a plan to fit every need."

One of the mountain men asks a question about insulation and Sherman gracefully hands it off to Clive. The audience, including the blue-eyed girl, turns to listen to Clive. Her neck is long and white. Sherman feels the beginnings of a hard-on. If he ever gets up the nerve to cheat on Josie, this girl is just the sort he'd like to poke. Sweet and soft. Probably smells up close like Ivory Soap.

At the end of the presentation, Josie invites the audience to come out the next day to the site of a log home they are building. "We believe that every log home we construct should result in the sale of other log homes," she tells them. A few people, including the blue-eyed girl and her husband, stop to sign up for the site visit and pick up a map. Sherman reads their names: Duane and Lolly Lunsford.

"Your kits are more expensive than Greenville Log Homes," Duane says.

"Shush, Duane," Lolly says, embarrassed.

Sherman risks a real wink this time. "Well, Duane, my answer to that is, anybody with a planer can manufacture a log, but it takes more than a stack of logs to make a home."

Lolly's smile shows little square teeth. Sherman usually lets Clive and Josie handle the site visits but he decides to go to the site himself tomorrow.

"Manager's looking for you," Clive says at his elbow. Sherman knows it's about money he owes the hotel from the last seminar they held there. When the audience is gone, he and Clive and Josie duck out a side door before the manager can corner them.

When he and Josie drive into their driveway Josie says tiredly, "The hot tub's clogged again. We're going to have to break down and call a plumber."

"When our cash flow gets a little better," Sherman says.

Inside, Josie washes off her mascara and touches peroxide to the roots of her hair. They go to bed without speaking. She wears a sleeveless nylon nightie. Her fleshy upper arms are rough with tiny pimples. Sherman's penis lies flaccid against his thigh. When he's sure she's asleep, he starts to touch himself, thinking about Lolly. The bed rocks gently as Lolly sweeps his stomach with her hair.

Sun at the construction site the next morning assaults Sherman's hundred-dollar genuine aviator sunglasses, bought in better times from the Home Shopping Network. Clive walks tight-lipped around him and Sherman feels the way he always does at a site — in the way. Lolly and Duane drive up around eleven o'clock in a beat-up 1974 Camaro that threatens to get stuck in the deep red mud left from clearing.

Josie reintroduces herself. "I'm Josie Rawl-Hall." She begins to explain the layout of the site. Sherman doesn't understand why she's gone to using a hyphenated name after twenty years of being just plain Josie Hall. Maybe she's thinking of leaving him, with the way things have been going lately, and the name change is just an interim step on her way back to being single. The thought raises his hopes and panics him at the same time.

"I'd be doing a lot of the work myself," Duane says, puffing a little.

"We admire the do-it-yourselfer," Sherman says.

"For the portions you might want help with, we can provide labor at $8 per square foot," Sherman says.

"That'd be a good idea on the roofing, Honey," Lolly says to Duane. "I don't want you falling off and leaving me to have this baby on my own." She touches her flat stomach.

"Are you expecting?" Josie coos. "No wonder you're looking to build a nice home."

Duane simpers, proud to have knocked Lolly up. Sherman eyes her tummy again. Knowing she's pregnant just makes him want her even more. He feels himself getting turned on and thinks fleetingly of what it would be like to take Lolly to the back of the half-built house and press himself against her, breathing in her smells along with the smell of cedar.

Clive leads them on a tour of the job site, the only site Sherman and Josie have where the customer isn't mad at them. Lincoln Log Homes owes its kit manufacturer $150,000. Outside licensed contractors have liens on the last three homes they've built. The money they get from new sales goes to pay old debts, not to purchase the kit the new customer has ordered.

Josie's main job these days is to make up excuses for why construction has been delayed.

As Clive explains the different ways logs can be fitted together, a sheriff's patrol car pulls up. Sherman slips away and meets the deputy at the bottom of the drive.

"You Sherman Hall?" the deputy asks.

"Yes, Officer. What can I do for you?"

"Got a summons and complaint for you, from a Jane and Thomas Radner." The Radners are the last couple Sherman ordered a kit for before the manufacturer cut him off. Clive got the foundation laid but Lincoln Log Homes hasn't been back to the site in five months.

"I'm sure there's just been some misunderstanding." Sherman glances up the hill. Lolly is looking at him in concern.

"Yeah, whatever. Sign here, please," the deputy says.

Sherman signs, and pockets the summons and complaint to read later. There's no point in taking it to their attorney. Sherman owes the lawyer so much money the guy won't take his calls.

He heads back up the hill. Clive is explaining why most people choose to drywall some rooms because they get tired of looking at cedar beams in every room. Josie stands close, ready to flatter Duane at every opportunity. Lolly trails behind.

"Is everything all right?" she asks him when he catches up with them.

"Absolutely," Sherman says with a wide smile. "The officer was just telling me some teenagers have been trespassing on this property—says we might want to secure our materials at night."

Reassured, Lolly turns back to listen to Clive.

Sherman has never liked confrontation, and the encounter with the deputy leaves him upset. Sherman can say that he made it to his thirties with no regrets. Then one day he looked back over his shoulder and here they came. He knows men his age who have children they can place their hopes in when their disappointments finally stop them in the road. Sherman has no children. His own fibs and failures eat away at him daily the way powder-post beetles attack untreated pine, leaving it porous and brittle. There is no part of his life anymore that feels whole and pure. He takes off his sunglasses and squints at the sun, blinking his eyes when they water.

"We got the sale," Josie tells him at home that afternoon. "They want either the Cape Codder or the Beach Comber. They'll let us know in the morning when they bring their check." She examines the complaint the deputy served that morning. "Not that it really matters what they want. It's not like we can deliver."

Sherman goes through the day's mail. One envelope is more ominous than the others, return address the Internal Revenue Service. He opens it. The letter tells him he owes $25,000 in back taxes and that if he doesn't pay, the IRS will seize his house and all business assets.

"How much are the Lunsfords bringing by tomorrow?" he asks Josie.

"Twenty-five thousand in a cashier's check," she says.

Sherman dreams of seducing Lolly. In his dream she has seen that Duane isn't man enough for her and has sought Sherman out for his wisdom and experience. She wears nothing. Her breasts are milk white and her stomach is just beginning to round as the baby grows inside her. Sherman wakes with a jerk and checks to see if Josie has noticed his irregular breathing.

Duane brings the check by at breakfast time, saying that Lolly is feeling sick to her stomach. Josie tells him morning sickness is natural. Sherman promises to order their Cape Codder kit this week. As Duane's Camaro backs out of the driveway, it starts to rain.

Josie goes back to bed to read a book. Sherman tries to wait out the rain. He fiddles with the clogged hot tub drain, with no luck. By late afternoon he sees that the rain will not let up. He pockets the IRS envelope and the Lunsfords' check, and heads out the door.

It's a ten-mile drive to the IRS office in Asheville. Rain hurls itself against the windows of Sherman's Bronco. His wipers are on high but even so he can hardly see. Traffic slows to forty-five miles per hour. More cautious drivers pull off to the side of the road to let the storm pass. Sherman holds tight to the steering wheel as his Bronco hydroplanes across a bridge and then regains traction. He passes a fender-bender on the other side of the highway and indulges thoughts of what would happen if he were killed in an accident. In a way it would be a relief. A clean crisp end to what has become a messy, complicated life.

Ahead of him a rusting maroon station wagon drifts too far to the left and catches a wheel on the ridge where pavement meets shoulder. The driver tries to correct, but loses control. The wagon travels a crease in the median until its front axle folds around a grassy mound of dirt. Sherman pulls over and backs up, more to delay his own errand than to be a good Samaritan.

He gets out and crosses to the grounded car, his feet squishing wet grass. Through the raindrops on the station wagon's window he sees a tired young mother, her mouth moving in curses. In the back seat a child of about two, scared by the impact, has his mouth open in a silent wail. The woman rolls down her window at Sherman's tap and the sound comes on. The child's screams echo up and down the highway, forcing Sherman to raise his voice to be heard. "Are you okay?" he asks.

"We're not hurt." The woman gets out, cell phone in hand as she looks at the damage. The little boy's screeches turn hysterical, pulsing out of him with every breath. Sherman worries that he might choke but the woman ignores him. She shakes her cell phone, as if trying to bring it to life. "Goddammit. No service. Just what I needed."

"My cell's in my car." Sherman turns to get his phone, glad that Verizon hasn't yet cut him off despite two threatening notices, but the woman passes him. "I'll make the call. My husband drives a tow truck.

Watch the baby for me, would you?" She is halfway to Sherman's Bronco before Sherman can respond.

Sherman climbs into the driver's seat of the station wagon and shuts the door against the rain. His knees bump the steering wheel. He checks the child in the back seat. The little boy is strapped in his car seat, hiccoughing violently. He wears nothing but a diaper, and from the smell of things it's time for a change. Sherman reaches back and unbuckles him, clumsily lifting him over to the front seat. He holds the little boy on his lap. The child shudders as he draws breath. Sherman puts a warm hand on his back and rubs in a circle, not knowing what else to do. "There, there," he says, expecting the child to start howling again, but by some miracle he quiets down. Sherman can smell the little boy's hair. He touches it and feels the scalp, warm and damp, underneath. The little boy sighs and sticks his thumb in his mouth. He settles back against Sherman's stomach. Sherman's legs stiffen and begin to ache from being crammed under the dash, but he doesn't move.

The child's mother opens the driver's side door, letting in rain. "All set. My husband will be here in half an hour." Her face softens for the first time. "Thank you for your help."

"Don't mention it." Sherman gently moves the little boy to the passenger seat and gets out of the car so the woman can get in.

"You don't need to stay. He's on his way," she says.

"Okay." Sherman raises a hand. "You all take care." He goes back to his own car and cranks it up. The interior fills with the smell of Johnson's Baby Powder and sticky toddler's breath.

At a pay phone across from the Federal Building, Sherman stops and looks up an address that lies eight miles north, up the mountain. Rain trickles down his beard and collar and dots the pages of the telephone book. Back in the car, steam rises from his clothing and fogs the windows. His Bronco, which hasn't seen a mechanic in two years because Sherman hasn't been able to afford it, takes him halfway up the mountain and quits. Sherman has four miles to go.

He makes sure the Lunsfords' check is safe in his jacket pocket. He flips his collar up around his neck and gets out, locking the car door behind him. Cold rain slaps his face so hard he can hardly breathe. Within seconds, water seeps through the soles of his worn Gucci shoes. He presses forward, one mile, then two. It starts to get dark. His calves ache with the uphill climb and he's glad there's no one around to hear the ragged in and out of his middle-aged breathing.

With one mile to go, he gets his second wind. He begins to feel pleased and proud of the thing he is doing. He stops minding the rain. At a mailbox that says "Lunsford," Sherman turns and marches his last fifty yards, up the cement block steps of a mobile home that sits in the yard of a leaning farmhouse.

The Camaro isn't in the yard but a light is on and he can hear Carrie Underwood's voice competing with the falling rain. He knocks on the door. Lolly opens it and looks at him, surprised. "Mr. Hall!"

"Sherman," he says. "Call me Sherman. I'm sorry to bother you, I just had to return this." He hands her the check, which feels damp and limp from his battle with the rain.

"Is there something wrong with it?" She holds the check up to the light. "The bank said it was guaranteed."

"There's nothing wrong with the check." Sherman tries to catch his breath without her realizing how out of shape he is. "It's just that our company is having some unexpected trouble getting all of our work completed on time. We've decided that instead of running the risk that we won't have your home finished on schedule, we'll just refer you to Greenville Log Homes." He wipes water from his face.

"You're really wet." Lolly touches his arm. "Do you want to come in and warm up?"

Sherman breathes in a fantasy of Lolly drying him off inch by inch and the two of them making love in the shadow of her in-laws' house while his clothes dry.

"No, thank you," he says regretfully. "I need to get back."

"All right, then." She gives him a parting smile and disappears into the trailer.

Sherman walks down the steps and back down the mountain. The rain finally starts to ease. A truck passes him, spattering his ankles. As he walks, Sherman recites the closing lines from his Lincoln Log Homes sales pitch. "All you have to do is pick a plan." He shakes water from his shoes. "Satisfaction guaranteed." He lifts his chin and watches the sky soften to a lighter gray. "We'll make your dreams come true."

**HEATHER NEWTON'S** debut novel, *Under the Mercy Trees*, won the 2011 Thomas Wolfe Memorial Award, and was chosen as a Great Group Reads selection by the Women's National Book Association and as an Okra Pick ("great Southern books right off the vine") by the Southern Independent Bookstore Alliance. An attorney and mediator, she has lived in Asheville since 1992 and never plans to move.

# Try Not to Think about It

An excerpt from *What I Came to Tell You*

TOMMY HAYS

*In this excerpt from my new novel, twelve-year-old Grover Johnston lives with his younger sister, Sudie, and their father in Montford, Asheville's historic neighborhood. Their mother, an elementary school counselor at Isaac Claxton where both Grover and Sudie attend, died in an accident several months earlier. It's now November.*

*Emma Lee and Clay Roundtree, a sister and brother from Spruce Pine, recently moved with their mother into the house across the street. Grover and Sudie are taking their new friends to downtown Asheville. Their final destination is the Thomas Wolfe House, which Grover and Sudie's father directs and which Emma Lee, a voracious reader and a big fan of Wolfe's novels, has wanted to visit.*

FRIDAY AFTERNOON, after school, Grover, Sudie, Clay, and Emma Lee walked down the front steps of Claxton Elementary and headed up Montford Avenue in the direction of the Wolfe House. Montford was a long wide street and the cold wind blew uninterrupted all the way from downtown. After a few blocks, they ducked into Reader's Corner to warm up.

The first thing Grover always noticed when he walked into Reader's Corner was the musty smell of used books. An old, comfortable smell. And even though he wasn't a big reader, being around books other people had read made Grover feel at home.

Byron, the owner, was a short, round woman with long white hair and spectacles perched on the tip of her nose—a female Benjamin Franklin. She sat at a desk surrounded by boxes of books, going through them and writing prices in pencil on the inside cover.

Grover took Clay over to the window to show him Tom, who pushed his head against Grover's hand and purred loud enough to hear across the store.

"Emma Lee's died and gone to heaven," Clay said. His sister stood in the middle of the store, taking in the shelves sagging with books.

"This is Clay," Sudie said to Byron, "and that's his sister, Emma Lee."

"Hey," Clay said. He turned back to Emma Lee. "Sis, we can't stay long."

Emma Lee, having already picked up a book, didn't say anything.

Clay leaned toward Byron and said in a low confidential tone, "She's a book-aholic."

Byron looked over her spectacles at Clay. "We get a lot of those."

Emma Lee disappeared around the corner of a bookshelf, still reading the book. "Uh-oh," Clay said, going after her. "Now Emma Lee . . ."

Watching Clay go after his sister, Grover remembered that one day he'd been behind her at Claxton and watched her walk down the hall, her long black hair swaying. It had taken his breath away. Up until that moment he hadn't really seen her, at least not like *that*. Now he'd be in the middle of doing homework or washing the dishes with Sudie or working in the Bamboo Forest, and suddenly there'd she'd be, walking down the hall at Claxton, her long hair swaying.

"How's the weaving going?" Byron asked. She was one of the few people he could talk to about his tapestries.

"I'd rather be in the Bamboo Forest," he said, still petting the cat. "But we're taking them to tour the house."

"It's kind of you to take time out for your friends. You always were a generous boy." She looked at him over her spectacles. "You come by it honestly." Grover wasn't sure if she meant his mother or his father. But Grover could never look into Byron's clear eyes anymore without seeing what she'd seen that warm evening last April just as she was closing her store: She had locked the front door and had been closing out the cash register, when there was a knock at the window. Grover's mother had been outside, waving in. She was always stopping to talk to Byron and buy a book or two. Byron had motioned for Grover's mother to come in and had started to unlock the door, but Biscuit was barking at Tom who had arched his back and hissed. Grover's mother had shaken her head and said, *I'm picking up a movie. I'll come by tomorrow without the dog.* She waved again and walked on. Byron heard sirens a little later but hadn't thought anything of it.

Grover never minded stopping by the Reader's Corner with Sudie. He wasn't interested in the books so much. He mostly liked petting Tom, talking to Byron, and looking through the very window where their mother was last seen alive.

After they left, they'd walked two blocks and the wind blew harder.

"I'm freezing," Sudie said shivering and looking longingly at Videolife as they passed by the store.

"Why don't we duck in there?" Clay said.

Grover stared at the store. "We've only got a few more blocks."

"Your sister looks cold," Emma Lee whispered into his ear.

Sudie's cheeks had turned holly-berry red. "For just a minute," he said.

With his heart pounding, Grover followed them inside. He hadn't stepped in here since the day their mother hadn't come home. Videolife was small, about a tenth the size of Blockbuster across town but had a lot more movies, especially old movies. The shelves, almost as close together as the ones in Reader's Corner, were packed with DVDs and old VHS tapes. Big handwritten signs dangled from fishing line above the sections: *Keep You Up at Night Scary, Too Deep for Us, Great Old Ones,*

*Strictly for Grownups, Okay for Everybody, Basically for Kids,* and *Stupid in the Stupidest Sense.*

On late Friday afternoons Grover and Sudie would walk down here, meet their parents, and decide on a movie together which wasn't always easy. They'd get take-out from a little restaurant called the Weeping Duck, then go home and watch the movie and eat wonton soup, egg rolls, and Grover's favorite, shrimp fried rice.

Sudie and Clay had gone straight to the *This Just In* section and found *Ratatouille.* They were reading what it said about it on the back of the DVD.

"Let me know if you need any help," said the guy behind the counter. He had a goatee and wore a turtleneck. He was watching a TV mounted high up on the wall in one corner where they always kept a movie playing. He was watching a Woody Allen movie. Their father loved Woody Allen. He would laugh at his movies. Most of the time, Grover didn't see what was so funny.

Sudie looked up at Grover hopefully, clutching *Ratatouille* to her chest. Grover shook his head. Sudie sighed and set it back on the shelf.

"It's just one little movie," she said. "I don't see what the big deal is."

And Grover wasn't about to tell Sudie why just the sight of his sister holding that DVD made him feel almost sick. He'd never tell her that his mother had asked him, when Videolife first called, if he would pick up the *Ratatouille* DVD that the store was holding for them after school. He'd never tell her that he'd forgotten about it till the day he'd seen their mother through the car's rear window, headed toward Videolife with Biscuit.

"Sure there isn't anything I can help you with?" The guy behind the counter glanced away from the movie for a second then went back to watching the TV.

"We came in to warm up," Grover said, standing by the door.

"Sure man," the guy said, not taking his eyes off the television. "Stay as long as you like. It's a mother out there."

*A mother?* Grover looked outside and then back at the guy who was caught up in the movie. He must've been talking about the weather.

They crossed the overpass that led into downtown, passing city work-ers who fought the wind to hang garlands, wreaths, giant yellow candles, and Christmas lights. They stepped into the Grove Arcade. In the entry-way, a red-cheeked man dressed in a Salvation Army uniform rang a bell for donations. Clay dug into his pocket, pulled out a crumpled dollar bill, and dropped it into the big hanging pot.

"Merry Christmas to y'all," the man said as the four of them walked on inside.

The first thing to hit them was the warmth, the feeling coming back into their hands and faces, as they looked at the long glistening hallway. Shafts of afternoon sunlight filtered down through the high windows, looking touchable.

"Monet," Emma Lee said to herself, staring down the hall.

"I gave the fellow a dollar," Clay said to his sister.

"Not *money*," she said impatiently. "The painter. It's like that painting by him." She looked down the hall. "Of the cathedral."

"Exactly!" Grover said looking at her. One year Grover'd given his mother a calendar of Monet's paintings.

Sudie showed Emma Lee and Clay the model in the middle of the building of how the architect had originally designed the building with a twelve-story tower in the middle, a small skyscraper. Grover had heard this story a million times, but it was only now that he thought what it must've been like for the architect. How disappointed he must've been to have worked so hard on something and created such a beautiful building on paper but never seen the whole thing built.

The arcade was busy with Christmas shoppers and people who'd come inside to get out of the cold. A group of shoppers had gathered in the center of the arcade where three musicians—a banjo player, a guitar player, and a fiddler—played old time Christmas music. The fiddler, a bearded man, had left his case open, and it was full of coins and dollar bills.

They played fast and hard. People tapped their toes and clapped in time. It was the kind of music that was hard not to smile to.

"Man, they're hot." Clay took off his backpack and started to clog.

"Clay's won the clogging competition at the Lamar Lunsford Festival every year since he was four," Emma Lee said.

"Look at that hillbilly go," said a well-dressed older man to a woman in a fur coat. Grover could tell from his accent that he was not from the South.

"My brother is *not* a hillbilly!" Emma Lee had whirled around and faced the man.

"I didn't mean anything by it." The man laughed and looked at his wife then back at Emma Lee. "I think your brother is one hell of a dancer."

"Don't call him a hillbilly," Emma Lee said, her jaw working.

"I really don't see the problem . . ."

"You heard the girl!" A man stepped up to the well-dressed man. Grover had noticed him standing behind them, listening to the music with his wife and two little blonde-haired girls. He had long hair, wore a ball cap and a hunting jacket.

"I didn't mean anything by it." The well-dressed man wasn't laughing now and his face had turned pale. "Tell him, Gertrude." He turned to his wife but she pressed her lips together as if this wasn't the first time her husband's mouth had gotten him in trouble.

"I wouldn't call nobody a hillbilly," the man in the ball cap said, leveling his eyes at the well-dressed man, "not if you expect to live a long and healthy life."

"Is that a threat?!"

"It's one of them health advisories."

The well-dressed man started to say something but seemed to think better of it. He took his wife's hand, and they disappeared through the crowd.

"'Preciate it," Emma Lee said to the man in the ball cap.

He gave her a wink and nodded toward the band. "The fella's right. Your brother's good." He stepped back and joined his family. Grover saw the sad look flicker across Emma Lee's face as she watched the man's little girls take their father's hands and lean back against him.

The band shifted into a faster song, and as the fiddle sped up, so did Clay's footwork. More people gathered to listen to the music and watch him dance. Emma Lee shrugged off her backpack and joined her brother. Other people stepped out of the crowd, joining Clay and Emma Lee, and pretty soon it seemed as if half the people in the Grove Arcade were dancing.

"Come on." Emma Lee waved Grover up.

He thought about going up, but his feet wouldn't move. He knew good and well that if his mother had been there, she'd have been dancing right in the middle of them.

Grover watched Emma Lee drink her hot chocolate. He didn't know if it was the cold or the dancing, but her cheeks had reddened and her eyes glistened. They had stopped in at Bean Streets long enough for Sudie to beat Clay in chess.

"Oh gross," Emma Lee was muttering under her breath.

A dreadlocked couple kissed and stuck their tongues into each other's mouths right in front of their table where Mr. Critt had hung a sprig of mistletoe on the tip of the mannequin arm coming out of the ceiling.

"Make me gag," Emma Lee said louder.

Grover laughed, nearly spraying hot chocolate everywhere.

"Don't knock what you haven't tried, sister," the dreadlock girl said to Emma Lee. She nodded toward the mistletoe. "Why don't you and your boyfriend give it whirl?"

"I'm *not* her boyfriend!" Grover said.

"Never too early to start," the dreadlock guy said, then, as if he was demonstrating, kissed the dreadlock girl another long kiss. The couple sauntered off toward their table in the back, his hand in her back pocket.

Grover couldn't bring himself to look at Emma Lee. He kept his eyes on the checkerboard as Sudie quickly finished off Clay. When he finally did look up, the expression on Emma Lee's face wasn't at all what he'd expected. He couldn't be sure but he thought she looked a little hurt.

"In case you hadn't noticed, my sister has a thing for Thomas Wolfe," Clay said, as Emma Lee ran ahead and disappeared into the Old Kentucky Home. Clay looked at the rocking chairs lined up on the long porch.

"The guests used to sit out here in the summers," Sudie said. "A long time ago, people stayed in boardinghouses like this when they visited Asheville. Now they stay in hotels." She pointed to the Renaissance Hotel, a huge, ten-story hotel across from the Wolfe House. Every afternoon, it threw the whole Wolfe House into shadow.

Inside, the first thing Grover noticed was the bright smell of pine and fir. Along the edges of the main exhibit room lay wreaths, a small stack of cut fir trees, and another neat pile of garlands made from pine branches. Emma Lee was already at the exhibits, stopping to read every word, something Grover hadn't done in all the years he'd come here. Little Bit and several of the tour guides draped garlands around the main room.

"He's in his office," Little Bit said, handing a garland to a tour guide on a ladder.

"You really are having a Thomas Wolfe Christmas," Sudie said.

Little Bit glanced off toward their father's office. "I thought your daddy would have a fit when he saw the bill. Instead, he said to make sure I got whatever I needed." She lowered her voice. "His mood has improved lately."

Grover walked to his father's half-open office door and found him standing at his desk with Leila Roundtree beside him. They were looking at an open book on the desk. The way they leaned together, almost touching, gave Grover an odd feeling. He knocked.

Leila and their father stepped back from each other.

"Come on in!" his father said. A tinge of red crept across his father's face. "I was showing Leila a first edition *Look Homeward, Angel.*"

When Leila Roundtree looked up from the book, it hit Grover how pretty she was and how she wasn't just somebody's mother. He thought about how his father had accepted rides from the Roundtrees in the mornings, how he and Leila had started going on walks after supper, how he came back from those walks in a good mood.

His father led the Roundtrees through the house, starting downstairs, taking them through the dining room, the kitchen, the piano parlor, the sunroom parlor, and then upstairs to the bedrooms. He showed them the room where Wolfe's brother Ben had died. Even without reading the book, Grover'd heard his father's spiel enough to know that Ben, Wolfe's older brother, was the angel in *Look Homeward, Angel.*

With no other visitors around, his father unhooked the velvet ropes and let the Roundtrees walk around in the rooms. Emma Lee hardly said a word the whole time. She seemed to soak it all in. One of the last rooms they visited was the bedroom where Wolfe's father died.

"This is the very bed he died in," Grover's father said.

"I'll be," Clay said.

"Was he like Gant in the book?" Leila asked.

"A funny guy," his father said, "full of life, quoted long passages of Shakespeare, built roaring fires, and on occasion given to excess."

"Given to what?" Clay asked.

"Drank too much," Sudie said.

As Grover's father led Leila and Clay on down the hall to another room, Grover noticed Emma Lee linger. She laid her hand flat on the bed where Wolfe's father had died. Grover came and stood beside her.

"They know of at least eleven people who died in this house," Grover said.

He heard his father's voice down the hall. Grover placed his hand on Gant's bed. "Course everybody who ever lived in this place is dead now."

Emma Lee looked at him.

"Wolfe's father. His mother. His brothers and sisters, all dead. Every boarder who ever stayed here's dead. And Wolfe's been dead since 1938."

"What are you saying?" Emma Lee asked.

Grover shrugged. "Just that everybody's dead."

"Or getting there," Emma Lee said.

Careful to replace the velvet rope, Grover led Emma Lee in the direction his father had taken Leila and Clay and Sudie, but found himself leading her down the hall toward the sleeping porch where Wolfe spent many nights and where he'd had to share the room with whatever boarder might be staying there at the time. It was Grover's favorite room because it had so many windows and was lighter than the rest of the house.

"He never knew from night to night where he'd have to sleep," Grover said. "Or who he'd have to share a room with." He pointed to the two beds that took up most of the room. "His mother was so cheap she'd squeeze as many beds into a room as she could. She even rented to people with tuberculosis. When he died of tuberculosis of the brain, they said he might've caught it from having to sleep in boarders' beds."

They could hear his father's voice down the hall, as he reeled off facts about Wolfe's seven brothers and sisters. Outside, the wind whistled and a loose shutter tapped against the house. Grover reached for Emma Lee's hand.

She looked at him and then down at his hand holding hers.

Her hand was warm and rough at the same time. He let go.

They didn't say anything. The wind whistled and the shutters tapped against the house. The two of them stood watching the wind in the bare trees and the light fading outside. Down the hall, their families' voices were coming toward them.

**TOMMY HAYS** is the author of *The Pleasure Was Mine*, a SIBA Fiction Award finalist. His other novels are *Sam's Crossing* and *In the Family Way*, winner of the Thomas Wolfe Memorial Literary Award. He is executive director of the Great Smokies Writing Program and a lecturer in the Master of Liberal Arts Program at the University of North Carolina–Asheville. His website is www.tommyhays.com.

# Chance Two

PAMELA DUNCAN

JAMES FOUND HIS UNCLE VICTOR at the shed, though shed was too fancy a word for it, really. It was a patch of ground by the woods where Victor had set his big work table, an old, cracked church pew, and a straight-backed chair under a waterproof canopy, with blue nylon tarps rolled and tied on each side for when it rained. He liked to go out there and smoke and work on his carving, said a man couldn't stand being cooped up in a house all the time. James figured the shed was really just Victor's way of having some place to his own self, somewhere to get away from Granny and Clinton and Carl. It was a little house to hold all those people.

As usual, Victor sat straight-spined in the chair, both feet planted on the ground, smoking his pipe. He didn't seem surprised to see James. "Hey son," he said and held out his free hand.

They shook and James sat on the pew. He kept his eyes moving, settling anywhere but Victor's face. He studied his own hands, rough as a cob, grease still under the nails from work. Meagan hated that, always wanted him to scrub and scrub before he touched his food, or her.

She acted like a mama already and the baby wasn't even born yet. She needed to remember she wasn't his mama.

"Mama called you," Victor said.

That pulled James's head up. "Yeah," he said.

The sweet pipe smoke drifted between them as they sat without talking, reminding James of when he was little and always wanted to do whatever his Uncle Victor did, even if it meant sitting still.

Victor took the pipe out of his mouth, studied the bowl. "They're sending the body next week," he said.

James jumped to his feet and walked to the table, ran his hands over the hunks of wood lying there. His uncle walked the mountain every day, searching out good wood, said it got harder to find every year. Every time he turned around, there was another bulldozer pushing over trees to build a gated community or a golf course. James picked up a block of hickory, turned and held it out for Victor to see. "What's this one going to be?"

"Don't know yet," Victor said. He tapped his pipe on the chair leg and rubbed the ashes into the dirt with his boot heel.

James picked up another piece, a long, skinny hunk of cherry. "Looks like a weasel," he said, tracing the smooth curves with his fingers.

"Otter," Victor said.

"What's the difference?"

"People in Asheville don't want no weasel on their coffee table."

"Yeah." James laughed. "How much you get for these things now?"

"Depends."

"On what?"

"Size. Type of wood. What kind of car the customer's driving."

James laughed again.

"I never take less than fifty. They got to really want it." Victor put his pipe in his pocket and came over to the table. He pried the lid off a Tupperware box and pulled out a Ziploc bag full of gray-green leaves. "How you liking your job these days, flatlander?" he said. He took a big pinch of leaves from the bag and pushed them into a little leather pouch with a string attached.

"Between my bossman and Meagan, I keep pretty busy," James said, craning his neck to look up at Victor, who had come to stand behind him. Victor put his hand on top of James's head and turned it to face forward. James felt like the first time his uncle had taken him to the barbershop. Sit up straight, don't ask questions, accept what is happening to you. Victor's arms came around his neck from behind. Then the pouch lay against his throat smelling like Granny's Thanksgiving dressing times a hundred. "What's this for?" James said.

"Call it medicine," Victor said.

"Medicine? What for?"

"For what ails you."

"Kind of strong, ain't it?" James said, rubbing his nose.

"That's the point."

That evening at supper, Granny and Clinton and Carl hardly said a word and wouldn't look James in the face. James wondered if they were ashamed, or maybe just scared. Either way, they went to bed early. In the living room, Victor and James sat side by side on the couch, pretending to watch a *Law & Order* marathon. By the end of the first episode, James couldn't stand it anymore. It was stupid to sit there pretending he was over it. "Just tell me one thing," he said, trying not to sound mad.

As if he'd been waiting for a sign, Victor raised the remote and put the TV on mute. "Shoot," he said.

"Why didn't nobody tell me he was alive?" James hated how he sounded like a five-year-old who didn't get what he wanted for Christmas.

"Because. You might've wanted to go see him some time."

"So?"

"The only way he was ever getting out was feet first. You didn't know him before he went in, and we decided you might as well keep on not knowing him."

James couldn't argue with that. He'd never even seen the man, except in pictures. "You could've told me after I got old enough, let me make up my own mind."

"Maybe we should have. But it's too late now."

"Did he not ever ask about me?" James said.

"No," Victor said. Then, as if to soften it, he said, "He never did."

James got up and walked over to the window. He shoved his hands in his pockets and stared into the pitch black on the other side of his reflection. His granny's cats were out there, squalling, fighting. The familiar sounds of the house—ticking clock, fire popping in the stove, snoring from the back bedroom—turned into a roaring in his head. He wanted to hunker down, just roll up in a ball and go to sleep, make it all go away.

Victor pulled on his shoulder. "Come on," he said, and James followed him outside.

In the shed, Victor set a little grill on the ground and started a fire with sawdust and scraps of carving wood. They sat on the pew and watched the flames, holding their hands to the warmth. In this in-between season, the time of warm days and cool nights, the last chance for crickets singing before winter set in, the cold seemed harder than it really was.

James pulled at the pouch around his neck. "Can I take this thing off now?"

"Sure," Victor said.

When James untied the string and held out the pouch, Victor pointed to the fire.

James did not feel like sitting on the cold ground, but figured he might as well get it over with. He slid off the pew and sat cross-legged in front of the grill, worked the pouch open and held it in both hands for a minute, then turned it upside down over the fire. The sage popped and burned as it landed in the embers, then began to smoke. As usual, he'd sat on the wrong side of the fire and the smoke blew right in his face. "Damn!" he said, coughing and gagging. "Damn!" His throat burned, and water streamed from his eyes and nose. He pulled the neck of his T-shirt over his face to mop it. The water and snot kept coming long after the smoke had cleared.

After a while, Victor spoke. "Your daddy . . ." he said. His voice deserted him. They sat still together a long time, listening to the wind in the trees. At last, Victor cleared his throat and spoke again. "Never mind him now. He's gone. Chance one, that's over. But you got something else now. You got Meagan and that baby. That's something. That's chance two, son."

Chance two. James hadn't thought much about being a father before. The baby didn't seem quite real yet, maybe because it still rested safe in Meagan's belly. But it was real. He was already a daddy. And this time, he would get it right. As long as he was alive, he had chances. James could almost feel sorry for his daddy. No more chances for him.

In pictures of when they were young, his daddy and Victor looked a lot alike — tall, skinny, grinning. Now Victor's face was a pale blur in the darkness, but James knew it by heart, the black eyes and wide mouth that hardly ever smiled but always looked like they wanted to, the face flat like pond water, so much going on under the surface. James stared a long time, wondering for about the millionth time how the man got so damn smart stuck on top of a mountain his whole life.

Then Victor's voice reached out to him. "Son," he said. "Ain't you got somewhere you need to be?"

---

**PAMELA DUNCAN** teaches creative writing at Western Carolina University. She has written three novels: *Moon Women* (a Southeast Booksellers Association Award Finalist), *Plant Life* (winner of the Sir Walter Raleigh Award for Fiction), and *The Big Beautiful*. She is the recipient of the 2007 James Still Award for Writing about the Appalachian South. Her website is www.pameladuncan.com.

# The Hills Beyond

# The Wolves in the Asheville Zoo

RON RASH

Fog grazing among the trees,
and they herd with it, become
whispers of movement until
one bares its throat, then silence
as though pausing for answer
from cliff-cave or laurel den
vacant twelve decades, and I
pause too, imagine the first
of my name in this county,
rock and wood raised on a ridge,
wind swaying the boards like waves
as if still inside the ship
sailing from land where wolfpacks
vanished far back as dragons,
denned deep in blood-memory until
given voice this mountain night
as oak slats rattle like bones,
the hearth's last log cools to ash
gray as his eyes as he pokes
charwood for some nub of light.

---

Novelist and poet **RON RASH** is the author of fourteen books, including the novels *One Foot in Eden* and *Serena*, which was a finalist for the PEN/Faulkner Award for Fiction. His most recent books are a novel entitled *The Cove* and a poetry collection entitled *Waking*. He teaches at Western Carolina University.

# A Mountain Garden

Excerpts from *Zoro's Field: My Life in the Appalachian Woods*

THOMAS RAIN CROWE

## *The Signs*

THE PEOPLE WHO REFER TO THEMSELVES AS NATIVES here in the mountains of Western North Carolina often do their planting, harvesting, and other garden-related activities by the signs. By "signs," I mean doing garden work in direct correspondence with the phases of the moon and the signs of the zodiac—the constellations in the sky. Many of these folks get their inspiration and information for this practice from the Book of Genesis in the Bible and a publication that is called *Grier's Almanac.* In Genesis, one finds the lines: "Let there be lights in the firmament of the heaven to divide the day from the night; and let them be for signs, and for seasons, and for days, and years." According to *Grier's Almanac* (which has been published annually since the early 1800s, and which is something of a secondary "bible" to farmers here in these mountains), going back as far as 1000 BC there are charts and records of the evenly spaced positions of the constellations in the firmament and the monthly path of the moon.

These observations were recorded and then divided into twelve parts, or "signs." Each sign was named for an animal and a corresponding part of the human body. Early astrologers used these charts in creating horoscopes and in the arcane art of soothsaying. This tradition has been carried down through the ages and with the help of the almanac has become a source of direction in the daily routines of people who consult it as a forecaster of weather, and as a guide for good planting and fishing days. They even turn to the almanac to determine when it is favorable to do such things as cut hair, kill weeds, and pull teeth. There are those I've encountered here in the mountains who consult the almanac daily before they do almost everything, as it is set up to be easily understood and used as a tool for divination.

Zoro introduced me to *Grier's Almanac* and to the idea of planting by the signs. Since it seemed to work for him, I got a copy from Pace's store and studied it, hoping to learn not only about its origins, but also about the secret to its apparent success. Over the past three years, I have tried this method of farming with varying degrees of success, and in the end I'm not sure that I understand it or believe in it any more than I did when I first attempted planting, cultivating, and harvesting in this manner. For instance, having derived from the almanac that the best time to plant is in one of the dry signs and when a dry day falls on both an ideal sign and an ideal phase of the moon, one year I planted my potatoes on a moonless night in March when the signs were not in the feet—the feet, bowels, and head not being particularly positive signs at this time of year. While I did get a good crop of potatoes that year, it was not the best crop I'd grown, and, in fact, was not as good as the crop I had the year before when I just planted them when it was convenient and the weather was good.

I've had similar mixed results with tomatoes—which are always a persnickety crop to grow. I dug my tomato holes according to the proper signs as indicated in the almanac (in the "new" of the moon, the first quarter), waited a goodly amount of time until the signs were propitious for planting the tomato slips that I had started from seed in my makeshift greenhouse on the south-facing side of the field, and planted them when the signs were in the hands—which predicted that there would be more flowers and less vine, and therefore a greater yield. That year I got the best crop of tomatoes I'd ever had—larger and with less blight. Well, the very next year I did exactly the same thing, using all the same signs in the same way at the same time, and, in comparison, got almost nothing for my efforts. And then this year I planted without consulting the signs and got another good crop.

My first year, Zoro told me to plant my corn when the signs were in the arms. "And whatever you do," he added, "don't plant any corn when the signs are in the bowels." His reasoning for this was: When the signs were in the bowels, the seeds would rot in the ground or be infected with impurities—just as food gets when passing through the body, from mouth to bowels. I did what Zoro said, and I got a good corn crop that year. But then the next year it rained all during the time when the signs were right, and so I planted my corn late. Even so, I got an equally good crop that year. So I'm still on the fence where this business of farming by the signs is concerned. Sometimes it works, and sometimes it doesn't. And sometimes it doesn't seem to make any difference. But since I'm here and living in a culture that largely embraces such a belief, I figure I'll do it this way, since it's tried and seems true for those from whom I am here to learn. What have I got to lose? Truth is, I've got a lot to lose living as close to the edge of things as I do. But, I'm game for trying new things and am susceptible to that which is odd, mysterious, or even downright *quar* (strange).

### Preservation

Almost all garden work is done with a single goal in mind: the preservation and storage of food. Food enough to carry me through the fall, winter, and early spring, when there is little, domestic or wild, that can be harvested or foraged for sustenance, such as nontoxic mushrooms, grapes or berries, wild greens or cresses, nuts or mast. Like many animals who work diligently in the fall to fill larder or bury foodstuffs, I set to work in the latter part of summer and continue into the month of September canning, drying, and storing various foods for the long, cold months ahead. My priorities and my focus reside on those crops that will sustain me and that I will be able to store, living as I do without non-natural refrigeration. Potatoes are stored in the wire and wooden crates in the root cellar. Winter squash (butternut, acorn, and buttercup) are stored, also in the cellar, in piles of straw. Apples are dried during the sun-bright, warm days of late September, outdoors, and then brought indoors and stored near to the woodstove, where they will be kept warm and dry. Beans, tomatoes, and applesauce are all canned in quart mason jars (which I've bartered for and gathered over the years) and stored on the rough-cut lumber shelves in the cellar. The long-keeper apples that I have culled from Mac's orchard, or over in the old orchard on the ridge road, are bedded in straw and kept in another of the wire and wood boxes in the cellar. Sweet potatoes are stored in burlap sacks behind the woodstove. Cornmeal is stored in anything I can find that will keep out the bugs and the damp. Jams, jellies, and honey (what the mountain folks call "sweetnin'") are canned in smaller glass jars and reside, too, in the cellar on their own shelf, like the aristocracy of all canned foods. Hearty cabbage, beets, turnips, and Jerusalem artichokes are left in the ground and covered in mulch, or sometimes stored in the root cellar if I can come up with some kind of container that will keep out pests and also allow the vegetables to breathe.

This assortment of vegetables and fruits is my larder, and from this meager list of foods I make my diet. A diet which is only as diverse as the list is long. But as repetitive as my eating habits are, they are also of the highest quality. One could even say gourmet. Gourmet in the sense that everything is more tasty and fresh than anything you could get in the grocery stores in town. And safer too. No noxious chemicals have tainted this food, as I have grown everything organically. I never tire of potatoes and green beans for dinner. Never tire of cornmeal grits and honey for breakfast.

Never tire of an apple and a piece of cornbread for lunch. Despite the repetition, each meal, like each new day, is a fresh start and a new experience for the palate. When writing about his garden and the food he ate in his cabin at Walden Pond, Thoreau penned philosophically: "Not that food which entereth into the mouth defileth a man, but the appetite with which it is eaten. It is neither the quality nor the quantity, but the devotion to sensual savors. I have been thrilled to think that I owed a mental perception to the commonly gross sense of taste, that I have been inspired through the palate, that some berries I had eaten on a hillside had fed my genius." While not able to write as eloquently as Thoreau about my meager larder, I would wager that I don't enjoy the fruits of my annual labor any less.

My organic and mainly vegetarian diet, supplemented occasionally with rabbit, squirrel (or other pilfering varmints that might try and fail at raiding my garden), fish from either the river or Johnson's Pond, and an occasional rattlesnake, has served me well these years. And I find that I don't suffer from any lack of protein manifesting in the form of waning energy or insufficient strength. I'm fit, strong, and well fed despite what some folks might think of as a dull diet. The dullness in my diet is what has allowed me to spend time doing the other necessary things that sustain me and my lifestyle here in Zoro's field. If things were any more complicated, I wouldn't have had time to chop wood and carry water, as the Buddhists would say.

In a simple diet it is a challenge to try and come up with new combinations, new recipes, to treat my palate, from time to time. "How many ways can you cook a potato?" someone once asked me during a conversation about my eating habits. "I'm only as limited as my imagination. And I've got a good imagination. A man's got to have a good imagination and a good sense of humor, living out in the woods alone. Needs these to keep yourself entertained, if not fed," I replied. And it's true. We are limited only by our own lack of imagination. I look forward each night to my plate of potatoes and beans. They not only keep me alive, but they are welcome company and companions to my hunger at the end of the day. The fact that I appreciate them all the more because I have grown them only adds to their inherent dignity and wonderful taste.

The topper for any woodland meal is a good glass of mountain spring-water. I suppose I drink at least a gallon of fresh springwater each day. During the summer months probably two gallons a day. A large glass of water with my midday meal or with my supper in the evening is as com-plementary as it is copacetic. One of Mac's favorite sayings in regard to the preservation of food from the garden is "Nothing less than first class!" By this he means that if it isn't a prime specimen of any fruit or crop, it won't be canned, stored, or eaten. Only the best parts of the apple are used for applesauce. Only untainted tomatoes are sliced to go into the pot for fixing stewed tomatoes. Only first-class carrots go into the stew. And water is the fine wine of the mountain recluse and aesthete. I would take to task anyone who might insinuate that "water is the poor man's wine." This is much too slanderous, for the flavor of good mountain springwater is every bit as engaging as any other drink you could find in a store. I haven't had a soft drink or any other sugared drink in over three years, and I can't say I've ever felt deprived. Vendors of popular and fast foods would have a hard time convincing me that what they sell is anywhere close to being as good as is the water that comes up from the ground in the holler beneath my field.

### Blue Ribbons

Using Mac's credo as a catalyst, this year I've taken the notion of first-class food a little further and in a much different direction than in years past. Instead of taking pride and pleasure in my harvested and canned food in ways that only come naturally and of necessity, I decided out of curiosity to take my best-of-the-best to the county fair. To see how my produce stacked up with that of folks living in the fast-paced world with all their modern conveniences. This impulse was as much a lark as anything else. Something bordering more on mischief than on a desire for recognition and accolade. I did it in order to play a Walt Johnson kind of prank on Mac. Since no monetary prizes were given for winners at the county fair, profit was not the motive for my conduct. It was just that I'd gotten good at growing things and going first class here in the woods, and I was ready to take the sharp hook of my learning curve and experience in the woods and drop it into the lake of the outside world and see what I could catch.

194

The largest county fair in Western North Carolina is held each year just outside of Hendersonville and represents the far-western counties of the state. By entering my produce, I'd be competing with farmers and suburban gardeners from ten counties. To say that I had no illusions about winning anything is an understatement. I simply wanted (for some reason unknown even to myself) to have my work there as part of the best of what the western part of the state had to offer, regardless of the outcome. "It's the journey that matters, not the arrival." So says the sixteenth-century French essayist, Montaigne. And it has been rephrased by many others for centuries since as koan or coda for the journey of how best to live one's life. For me, with regard to the Western North Carolina Agricultural Fair, it was in the entering, not the winning, that mattered. Or, at least this was what I was leading myself to believe.

I figured that if I was going to take the trouble to do it at all, I might as well do it big. In the end, and as the punch line for my prank, I made labels for the canned goods I was entering that read: "McHugh Farms." Mac would have never authorized such an action, but I took the liberty and caught a ride to Hendersonville with Saluda native Paul Rhodes who had come out to see how my bees were doing. Not only did I take samples of my canned applesauce, green beans, tomatoes, and some passion fruit jelly, but I also took a couple of sunflowers that had just come into full bloom, gourds, and my largest acorn squash. I had a tote sack plumb full, as Zoro would say, and I felt a little like Dorothy, departing for Oz.

Two weeks later, I returned to the fairgrounds and came home with a slightly less bulging tote sack but with a handful of ribbons. When Paul let me out of the truck on the old ridge road, instead of heading over the hill toward the cabin, I went straight up the hill in the direction of the McHugh farm. On the big table on the back porch, I put the canned goods with their McHugh Farms labels. Next to each of the winners, I placed the ribbon. For the green beans: yellow (second place). For the applesauce: blue (first place). For the canned tomatoes: white (third place). For the passion fruit jelly: blue (first place). For the wildflower honey: blue (first place). As well as winning ribbons for my canned entries, I had also won a first premium blue ribbon for my sunflowers as part of the flower show competition, and a second premium yellow ribbon for a couple unusual Dinosaur gourds that I'd raised from seeds given to me by an elder over on the Cherokee Reservation.

I laid all the ribbons out on the table and quietly slipped off the porch and walked back down the hill and across the road and over another hill to the cabin. When I returned to the McHugh porch later in the day—when I knew Mac would be there having his end-of-day drink of scotch and water—he greeted me not with an expression of displeasure for having used his name in vain, as it were, on the labels of the canned vegetables and jellies, but rather with a large smile. He said nothing. Just smiled. I think that, although he didn't say it, he was just as pleased as I was that we'd run the table at the WNC Fair with food and flowers grown on his land. Even now, some months later, the string of ribbons won at the fair is hanging up like hunting trophies in his canning kitchen in the old converted barn, where he can see them whenever he passes by.

*Planting Corn*

When the moon
beds warm and silver in the sky, and
the signs are in the hands:

it's time to plant corn!

When crow starts
in spring with his breakfast songs
and cotton meal lies golden in the row:

it's time to plant corn!

As the bluebird feeds
its first batch of young and
the sky takes earth in hand,
and I dance in the darkness of
a moonlit field where spring now rules the land
to the tune of Kanati's horn:

plant corn!

---

**THOMAS RAIN CROWE** is the author of numerous books. His nonfiction work includes *Zoro's Field, The End of Eden: Writings of an Environmental Activist,* and *Rare Birds: Conversations With Legends of Jazz and Classical Music.* His fiction includes *A House of Girls.* He has also published several collections of poetry, most recently *Crack Light.* He is founder and publisher of New Native Press.

# Et in Arcadia Ego

KEITH FLYNN

When the trees bow
and bushes curtsy, as
the silk wind brushes
through my bramble-
cluttered garden, the
claws of the field mice
and piston-powered
rabbits scramble the
unbroken dirt, the
untended roses groan
under the weight of
their thorns, the
untethered tomato vines
sprawl and dump their
fire-red loads among
the robust weeds.
At one corner, Japanese
hornets have assembled
a gray colony the size
of a watermelon and
ward off semi-serious
excursions to pluck
a renegade bud or

puckered potato already
on the verge of rot.
A toxic black walnut
tree stands sentinel
at the leaning gate,
dropping its dark
grenades into the field's
jumbled stalks. Two
squirrels quarrel over
which one should
command this wasted
circle first, the entire
acre fat on my neglect.

---

**KEITH FLYNN** is the author of five books—four volumes of poetry, including *The Talking Drum* and *The Golden Ratio*, and an essay collection, *The Rhythm Method, Razzmatazz and Memory: How to Make Your Poetry Swing*. His poetry and essays have appeared in many journals and anthologies, including *The Colorado Review, Poetry Wales, The Southern Poetry Review*, and *Shenandoah*. He is founder and managing editor of *The Asheville Poetry Review*.

# "Beautiful world, farewell!"

## The Story of John Lyon:
### Scottish Explorer, Plant Hunter, and Nurseryman

GEORGE ELLISON

ASHEVILLE IS SITUATED in the heart of the southern Blue Ridge geographic province. Whatever else it may claim to be, the city has always been defined by the ready access it provides to scenic views and a diverse flora unsurpassed in the temperate regions of the world. Purple rhododendron, fetterbush, pinkshell azalea, Fraser magnolia, Blue Ridge St. John's-wort, Oconee bells, wretched sedge, Appalachian avens, mountain dwarf dandelion, gayfeather, granite dome bluets, Fraser's sedge, Rugel's ragwort, and Blue Ridge goldenrod are but a few of the plants whose native ranges are primarily restricted to the neighboring mountain ranges where fifty or so peaks exceed 6,000 feet in elevation.

Following in the footsteps of botanists William Bartram, the father-and-son team André and François Michaux, and John Fraser, and soon to be followed by Thomas Nuttall, Asa Gray, and Moses Ashley Curtis, among others, John Lyon (1765–1814) was one of the plant collectors who ventured here during the late eighteenth and early nineteenth centuries to catalog the flora. Despite the fact that the genus *Lyonia* is named in his honor, Lyon is perhaps the most neglected of those mentioned above. An overview of his activities and of his death in Asheville (where his gravesite can still be located) is worthy of notice by those interested in the region's storied botanical history.

Lyon was born in Gillogie in Forfarshire, Scotland, a center of flax production. Little is known about his early life or about events that brought him to the United States. By 1796, he was managing the 300-acre garden of William Hamilton located on his Woodlands estate alongside the Schuylkill River just outside Philadelphia. Beginning in 1799, in order to secure additional plants for Woodlands, Lyon was commissioned to make a collecting trip into the Allegheny Mountains of central Pennsylvania. Thereafter until the year of his death, so as to pursue personal interests and financial security, he made excursions as far west as Nashville and as far south as Florida. Most of his travels, however, were in the southern Appalachians, especially into Western North Carolina, which he visited on seven separate occasions. Asheville became his home away from home.

A journal Lyon kept is preserved in the American Philosophical Society in Philadelphia. It was edited with extensive notes by Joseph and Nesta Ewan and published in 1963 as *John Lyon, Nurseryman and Plant Hunter, and His Journal, 1799–1814*. The journal indicated that Lyon collected plants atop several of the region's high peaks, including Roan, Grandfather, and Pilot mountains in North Carolina.

He is credited with introducing more than thirty new plants into horticulture. Among these was fetterbush (*Pieris floribunda*), which he discovered in 1807. Fetterbush, now planted as far north as Boston because of its hardy nature, is prized for its handsome habit and beautiful early floral displays.

In *A Reunion of Trees: The Discovery of Exotic Plants and Their Introduction into North American and European Landscapes*, Stephen A. Spongberg recalled that Lyon was the last person to observe and collect the famed Franklin tree (*Franklinia alatamaha*) in the wild. That was on June 1, 1803, while botanizing the region west of Savannah, Georgia.

Lyon was inordinately successful in transporting living plants to England because he established selected garden sites in the Philadelphia area where they could be maintained prior to bulk shipment. Although he sometimes had commissions for certain species from wealthy patrons, he sold his stock primarily at auction. Spongberg described a closely printed, 34-page catalog published by Lyon in 1806 prior to one such auction at Parsons Green in London. The catalog "enumerated 550 lots, and the sale occupied four days. Several of the lots were composed of large quantities of one-year-old seedlings in pots; and ten lots at the end of the sale consisted each of 50 different sorts of seeds."

John Loudon, a Scottish chronicler of arboriculture and agriculture, hailed this shipment in his *Arboretum et Fruticum Brittanicum*, published in 1838, as having been "by far the greatest collection of American trees and shrubs ever brought to England at one time by one individual."

Spongberg, himself a noted collector-naturalist in China and elsewhere, described with evident sympathy "the risks and privations encountered in the field" by innumerable collectors through the ages. Lyon's situation, in this regard, was extreme:

> On one foray a mad dog bit the collector on the leg, forcing Lyon to sear the three punctures he sustained with a burning-hot iron and to depend on self-administered folk remedies. When his horse went astray he was sometimes forced to travel on foot, and poor roads and the lack of maps or adequate directions often resulted in lost bearings and restless nights spent without an evening meal and the comfort of a bed. The ultimate disaster that can befall the collector-naturalist in the field is to meet an untimely death, thousands of miles from home, family, and friends. This was the fate of John Lyon.

That fate is described in the second volume of F.A. Sondley's *A History of Buncombe County, North Carolina* (1930), wherein a letter written in 1877 by historian and agriculturist Silas McDowell is reproduced. Primarily a resident of Macon County, North Carolina, McDowell lived as a boy from 1812 to 1814 near Asheville. In this letter, McDowell noted that, due to a "bilious fever" contracted during his strenuous travels, Lyon — "a low, thick-set, small man of fine countenance" — came from Black Mountain in the early autumn of 1814 and took a room in the Eagle Hotel. McDowell's description continued:

> Just below Eagle street stood and still stands the building then and for years afterwards known far and wide as the Eagle hotel, then owned by James Patton and later by his son James W. Patton. There were a large blacksmith shop just below this hotel, where Sycamore street now leaves South Main, and a tannery on the branch back of and below this. Joshua Roberts lived on the hill where Mrs. Buchanan lived until her recent death, and it was the last house on that side of the street. This was built by the late James Patton, father of the late James W. Patton, and grandfather of the late Thomas W. Patton. He was born in Ireland February 13, 1756, and came to America in 1783. He was a weaver, but soon became a merchant. In 1791 he met Andrew Erwin, who married his sister and became his partner in business. In 1807 they moved to the Swannanoa at what is known as the Murphy place, where they remained till 1814, when they moved to Asheville, Mr. Patton opening a store and the Eagle hotel — the central or wooden part. In 1831 he bought and improved the Warm Springs, and died at Asheville September 9, 1846. James W. Patton was born February 13, 1803, and died in December, 1861. His life was full of good deeds. His son, Thomas W. Patton, was foremost in all good works, and in 1894 came to the rescue of Asheville in a crisis of her affairs as mayor on an independent ticket.

According to McDowell, Lyon and James Johnston, a blacksmith of "almost Herculean" size from Kentucky, had become friends during the botanist's earlier visits to Asheville. When Lyon took to his sick bed,

Johnston had another bed placed in the same room for his own use and attended the botanist at night, "waking from what seemed to be a profound sleep at the slightest movement of the invalid" and taking him "in his large muscular arms and handle him with as much ease as a mother does her infant."

McDowell had also become attached to Lyon, and on the day of his death went to his room earlier than usual. Well over half a century later, McDowell recalled:

> This day had been one of those clear autumnal days when the blue heavens look so transcendently pure! But now the day was drawing fast to a close, the sun was about sinking behind the distant blue mountains, its rays gleaming through a light haze of fleecy cloud that lay motionless upon the western horizon. . . . The dying man caught a glimpse of the beautiful scene and observed: "Friend Johnston, we are having a beautiful sunset—the last I shall ever behold—will you be so kind as to take me to the window and let me look out?" Johnston carried him to the window, took a seat and held the dying man in a position so that his eyes might take in the beautiful scene before him. . . . After the sun sank out of sight, and the beautiful scene faded out, he exclaimed: "Beautiful world, farewell! Friend Johnston lay me down upon my bed". . . . He fell asleep in a short time and soon all was still. All of John Lyon that was mortal was dead.

Soon after Lyon's death, his friends in Edinburgh, Scotland, shipped to America an engraved tombstone that now marks his grave in the Riverside Cemetery in Asheville. There he rests with such literary luminaries as Thomas Wolfe and William Sydney Porter (O. Henry), as well as significant figures in other fields like Zebulon Baird Vance, Thomas Clingman, and George Masa. According to an extensive "Riverside Cemetery Walking Tour" compiled by cemetery manager David Olson, Lyon's grave had originally been in the old burial ground at the corner of Market and Eagle streets but was subsequently moved to the old Presbyterian graveyard on Church Street, and finally to the Riverside Cemetery. The marker was for many years thought to be the oldest engraved tombstone in Western North Carolina, but recently several older engraved tombstones have been located in Asheville.

From Gillogie in Forfarshire, Scotland, to Asheville in the Carolina mountains, collecting plants in all weather and under dire circumstances, it was for the explorer-collector-nurseryman John Lyon a long strange journey—one that, for the most part, he apparently reveled in until the very end.

GEORGE ELLISON writes the Nature Journal column for the *Asheville Citizen-Times*; the Botanical Excursions column for *Chinquapin: The Newsletter of the Southern Appalachian Botanical Society*; and the Back Then column for *Smoky Mountain News*. Collections of his nature writing include *A Blue Ridge Nature Journal* and *High Vistas: An Anthology of Nature Writing from Western North Carolina and the Great Smoky Mountains* (two volumes).

# About the Cover

The cover illustration for *27 Views of Asheville* is the work of Chapel Hill writer and artist Daniel Wallace. His illustrations have appeared in many publications, including the *Los Angeles Times, Italian Vanity Fair,* and *Our State Magazine.* He also illustrated the book covers of *27 Views of Hillsborough* and *27 Views of Chapel Hill,* both also published by Eno Publishers.

# Award-winning Books from Eno Publishers

*27 Views of Chapel Hill*
A Southern University Town in Prose & Poetry
INTRODUCTION BY DANIEL WALLACE
$16.50 / 240 pages

*27 Views of Hillsborough*
A Southern Town in Prose & Poetry
INTRODUCTION BY MICHAEL MALONE
$15.95 / 216 pages
Gold IPPY Book Award, Best Anthology
Gold Eric Hoffer Book Award, Culture

*Chapel Hill in Plain Sight*
Notes from the Other Side of the Tracks
DAPHNE ATHAS
$16.95 / 246 pages

*Undaunted Heart*
The True Story of a Southern Belle & a Yankee General
SUZY BARILE
$16.95 / 238 pages
Silver IPPY Book Award, Best Regional Nonfiction

*Brook Trout & the Writing Life*
The Intermingling of Fishing & Writing in a Novelist's Life
CRAIG NOVA
$15.95 / 152 pages

*Rain Gardening in the South*
Ecologically Designed Gardens for Drought,
Deluge & Everything in Between
HELEN KRAUS & ANNE SPAFFORD
$19.95 / 144 pages
Gold Book Award, Garden Writers Association
Silver Book Award, Garden Writers Association
Silver Benjamin Franklin Book Award
Honorable Mention, Eric Hoffer Book Award

Eno's books are available at your local bookshop and from www.enopublishers.org